Victorian &
Edwardian
Somerset

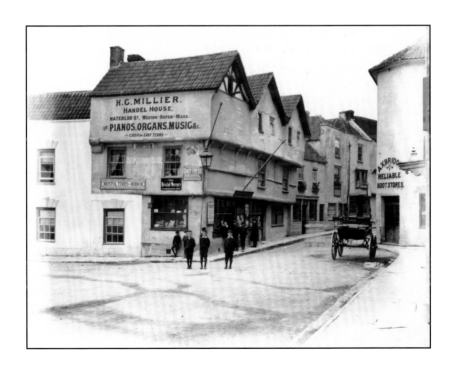

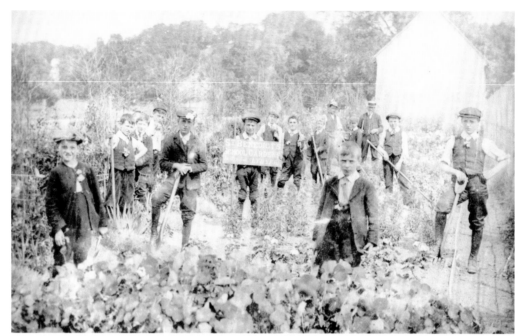

ST BENEDICTS SCHOOL, GLASTONBURY

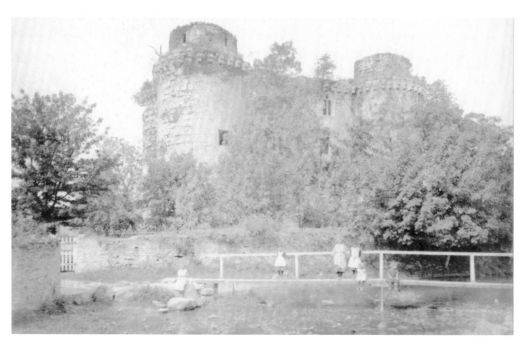

NUNNEY CASTLE

Victorian &
Edwardian
Somerset

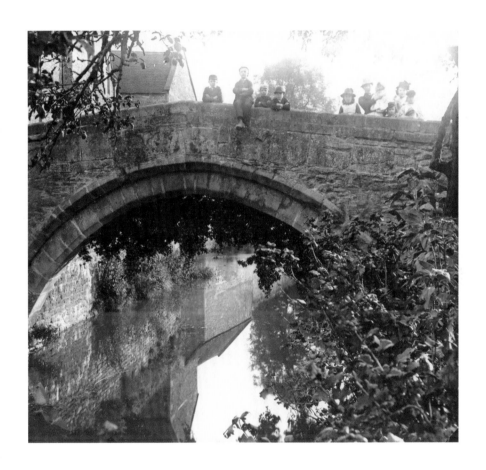

Robert Dunning

AMBERLEY

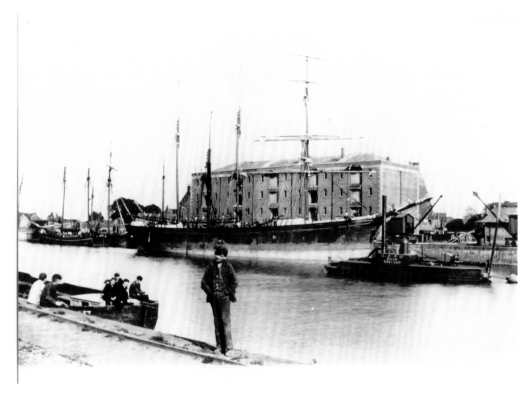

BRIDGWATER DOCK

First published 1993 under the title *Somerset of 100 Years Ago*
This revised edition first published 2008

Amberley Publishing
Cirencester Road, Chalford,
Stroud, Gloucestershire, GL6 8PE

British Library Cataloguing in Publication Data.
A catalogue record for this book is available from the British Library.

ISBN 978-1-84868-026-5

Typesetting and origination by Amberley Publishing
Printed in Great Britain by Amberley Publishing

Introduction

The extracts which form the text of this volume are taken from a variety of sources—monographs, essays in collections, articles in magazines, almanacs, published letters and diaries, and unpublished journals. The monographs range in style from the formal record of a mayoralty—that of George Woodiwiss, mayor of Bath 1896–7, published privately and handsomely to record an eventful year both in the life of the mayor himself and of his proud city; to the light-hearted and endearing prose of Alfred Percivall, alias the Revd Alfred Percivall Pott, who retired from parish work to the rural idyll of Buckland St Mary in the late 1890s.

In time the extracts begin in the early 1870s with the passionate investigative journalism of F.G. Heath for whom the rural idyll was a figment of the imagination. Exactly contemporary are the almost laconic diary entries of Francis Kilvert on holiday with members of his family at Weston-super-Mare and with friends in Taunton. Also from the same years comes the journal of the Revd Sydenham Hervey, hard-working curate in Bridgwater but also son of the diocesan bishop.

Later in the 1870s there are pieces by 'Church Rambler', an anonymous regular contributor to the *Bath Herald*, whose principal aim—to describe church services he attended—was often so delightfully accompanied by some spirited animadversion on architecture or some practical comment on the village scene.

The 1880s are represented by Richard Jefferies, straying from his beloved Wiltshire for a long article on 'Summer in Somerset' which appeared, accompanied by drawings by J. W North, in an issue of the *English Illustrated Magazine* of 1888. The less well known Theodore Compton's *Winscombe sketches amongst the Mendip Hills* was enough in demand for a second edition in 1882. These are very much tourist literature of the best kind; pieces for those with taste and leisure, the armchair walkers willing to be entranced and even mildly stimulated by the idea of a summer ramble but not alarmed by the energy and excitement of Mr Jerome and his companions.

The words of Cuming Walters, Charles Press and Walter Raymond suggest that the readers of the 1890s might well—so many branch railway lines were there in Somerset—find that a visit to a literary shrine or the achievement of a consummate view might be within the realms of possibility, but on no account must vulgar enthusiasm be allowed to intrude: such folk were still idlers—the name of one of the literary effusions to which Raymond contributed—though the piece included here was for those subscribers who recognized themselves as Idlers out of Doors.

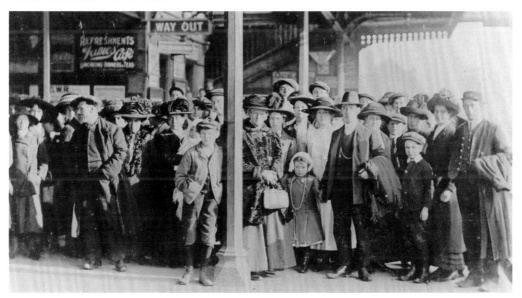

BRIDGWATER STATION

But not all was idling in the 1890s. 'Parochial Improvements' recorded in the *Diocesan Kalendar* were evidence of much activity in the life of many parish churches, and the social whirl of Castle Cary as recorded in the *Visitor* left no time at all for real leisure. The farming community, forced to mechanize to survive, was active too, in 1893 playing host to dairy farmers from all over the country and proudly exhibiting the cheese school at Butleigh and the dairy factory at Evercreech.

And there was no idling in the year 1897. George Woodiwiss, so young and so new to Bath City Council, was chosen mayor for Diamond Jubilee Year precisely because of his energy; the right man (with a suitably deep pocket) to uphold and even enhance civic dignity in that momentous year. Politics were laid aside; the Queen-Empress was the focus of attention in city, town and village. Teas, sports, bonfires and medals were all rather ephemeral though no doubt long remembered; more permanent memorials were a church organ, a nursing home, pleasure gardens or recreation grounds.

The Diamond Jubilee recalling sixty years of a memorable reign turned back the minds of many. Those sixty years had witnessed social and political changes which had revolutionized education and local government. Squire and parson may still have dominated the village scene but parish and county councils had come alongside the Poor-Law Guardians as organs of public authority and the village school was beginning its attack on rural ignorance and rural speech. Llewelyn Powys dilated nostalgically on his early years in an idyllic Montacute where his father was vicar, but his was a distant view; by the time he wrote, the Phelipses had left the Big House; Pitt Pond of his childhood was a derelict marsh. Distant, though not so distant, was the view of Alfred Percivall. His shepherd on the Blackdown Hills had probably gone by the time he wrote, although his recollection makes Silas Noldart ring delightfully true. Walter Raymond accurately recorded local speech in all his writing but W. Cook's Tommy Nutty was, perhaps, a little forced, though at the time very popular. The fear that 'the universal spread of education' would 'efface all interesting local peculiarities and bring the entire population to the unpicturesque level of a Board School Teacher' was a real one—and rather flattering to the teaching profession. Television is doing what schools failed to do a century earlier, but today's version of the language is no nearer a universal mean than was the Somerset dialect of the 1890s.

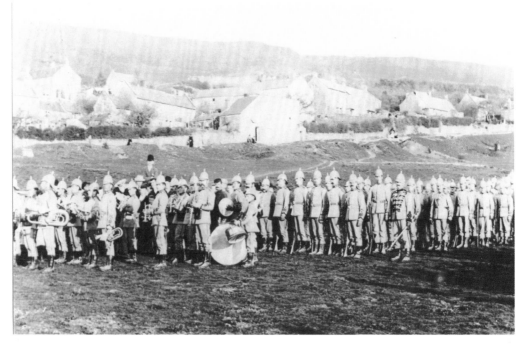

VOLUNTEERS, STOKE SUB HAMDON

The world of 1900 was far from Kilvert and Sydenham Hervey and F. G. Heath, and in two decades it was to change still more. The house party like that at Mells Park described by Raymond Asquith did not end abruptly as did so much else in the carnage of the First World War, but the thousands of personal tragedies in which Somerset families were engulfed resulted in a social revolution in which the political and economic influence of the owners of such houses began to weaken. After the destruction of so many gallant lives, the labouring peasant and his speech could no longer be the objects of idealism and mild amusement. He had fought in the trenches for his country, and it was entirely reasonable that those few who returned should have paid holidays and a chance to idle in their turn. The country house family increasingly found subservient staff hard to come by.

At a greater distance, nostalgia has an important place. Many of the extracts chosen come from ephemeral publications whose potential value someone recognized. Charles Tite of Taunton, an active Secretary of the Somerset Archaeological and Natural History Society, devoted much energy to collecting books, articles and pamplets, a task in which the most tenuous links with the county, a task in which he was ably assisted by at least one Bristol librarian. The resulting Tite Collection, owned by the Archaeological Society, contains the majority of these pieces and, of course, many more of the same kind.

The same society is owner of about one third of the originals of the photographs here printed, most of them in the form of glass negatives of varying sizes. Such has been the rather haphazard nature of the society's collecting that very few of the photographers are known by name, though that of Dr F.J. Allen should be recorded. His plates, still kept in their original envelopes, record in precise detail the particular photographic process each has undergone.

Allen was the gifted amateur pursuing a passion across the county, wherever his fellow antiquarians took him and beyond. The gentlemanly pursuit was evidently joined by a Duckworth of Orchardleigh and a Southcombe of Stoke sub Hamdon, the one capturing pastoral scenes in his wide home acres, the other the busy village whose women cut and sewed in his factory to produce gloves by the hundred dozen. Here, too, are represented the professionals: inevitably the ubiquitous Francis Frith but equally inevitably, when the eye strays towards West Somerset, the fine plates of H.H. Hole.

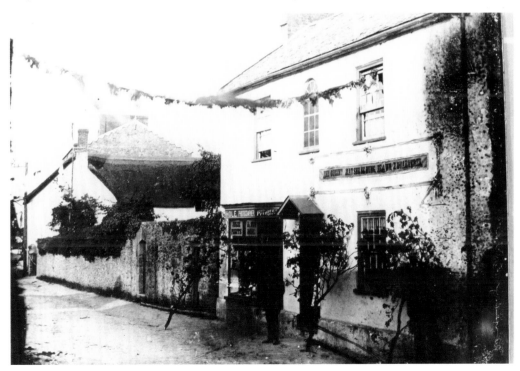

H. H. HOLE, PHOTOGRAPHER, WILLITON

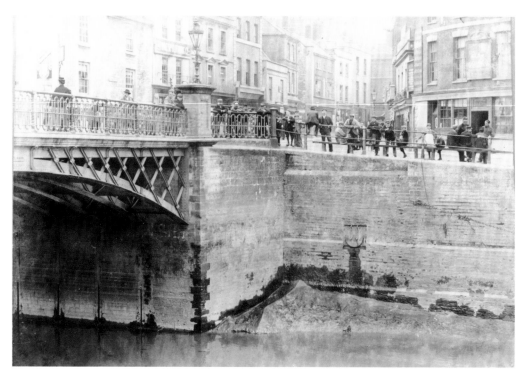

BRIDGWATER BRIDGE

Allen's passion, entirely appropriate for a Somerset antiquarian, was church towers, and the products of his anonymous fellow-photographers in the collection are similarly biased towards buildings. Buildings do not move. The photographs in this volume can hardly be expected wholly to illustrate the words; who was there with his camera to capture the peasant in his darkened hovel? The camera could not have coped with the dark and the photographer would not, in any case, have been welcomed.

So technological limitations must be accepted, the blur of a fluttering flag or a wriggling child must be seen as a normal hazard. But no wonder the photographer was allowed but two exposures after the Hervey wedding at Wells; today's albums would have taken all day. The consequence is that many in the collection are rather formal compositions, even the busiest workmen stopping to lean nonchalantly on their tools. But still, though they pause for a moment or two, they are at work or on their other lawful occasions—railway porters and railway passengers, quarrymen and geologists, carter with horse and putt and proud car owner. True, most streets seem to be full of people suddenly come to a halt and all facing in the same direction, but who would not stand and stare at a man with a tripod and black cloth?

And, as one ought to expect, there are idlers—leaning over the rails by Bridgwater bridge; idlers out of doors by the village shop, or in town at a royal Proclamation. And if not idlers, then folk on holiday attending a seaside horse-race or an archaeological society excursion, a meeting with fellow Primitive Methodists, the Club Day Walk, the militia camp. The hilarity of a house party was not, of course, quite suitable for pictorial publication; the new lodge and imposing entrance gates kept prying lenses at bay, but the portrait photographer with the proper address and the right connections might occasionally be offered his lordship's patronage. The camera has a way of revealing what the pen will often disguise; together they are a formidable combination.

Robert Dunning
Taunton
June 1993

Victorian
& Edwardian
Somerset

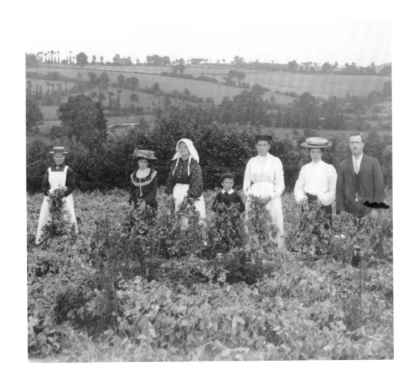

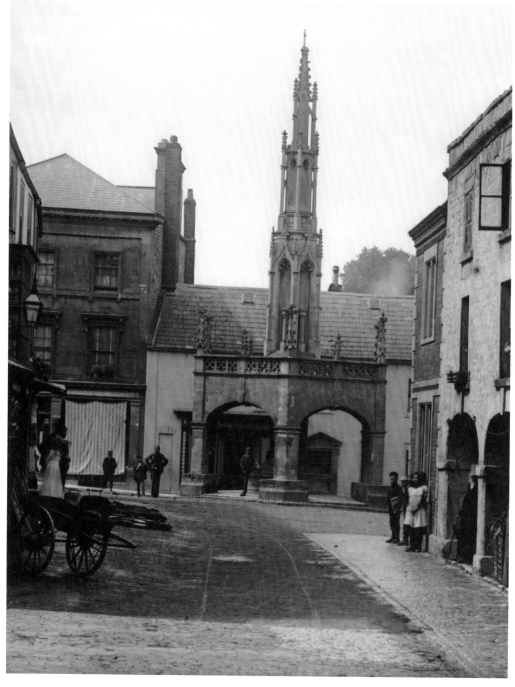

MARKET PLACE, SHEPTON MALLET

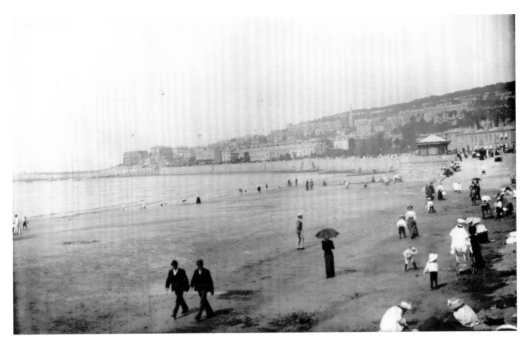

WESTON-SUPER-MARE

SEASIDE

Tuesday, 3 September 1872

At 9.20 I left Chippenham to join the rest of the party, my mother, Dora, and the children Katie and Monk, at 1 Prince's Buildings, Weston, leaving my Father and Fanny alone at Langley.

I found Thersie and Florence at Prince's Buildings. She has lodgings just above at 14 Manilla Crescent.

In the evening I had a bathe in the open sea for the first time for ten years and enjoyed it thoroughly.

We went to the new Pier which connects the mainland with Birnbeck. The 3 children were with us and the sea air seemed to make them wild. They grew so excited, they ran and shouted and screamed and rolled about on the pier tumbling over and over one another. . .

Wednesday, 4 September

Bathing in the morning before breakfast from a machine. Many people were openly stripping on the sands a little further on and running down into the sea, and I would have done the same but I had brought down no towels of my own.

At 7 o'clock this evening my Mother, Dora and I walked up to Trinity Church and heard Mr Hunt preach. During the service the lightning looked in at the windows and shamed the gas while from the town far below came up on the still sultry air the strains of the Italian band.

Thursday, 5 September

I was out early before breakfast this morning bathing from the sands. There was a delicious feeling of freedom in stripping in the open air and running down naked to the sea, where the waves were curling white with foam and the red morning sunshine glowing upon the naked limbs of the bathers.

Friday, 6 September

From Wells I went on to Glastonbury, a 12 minutes journey. There was a much larger and more important town than I expected to find, a bright clean cheerful-looking town on the slope of a gentle hill and two fine church towers, St John's and St Benedict's. It was some little time before I found out the old Abbey which lies back from the street behind some houses.

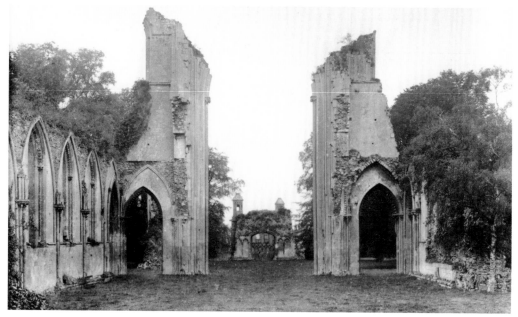

GLASTONBURY ABBEY

At the Porters Lodge the kindly woman showed me a long stout black holly staff which was found in the stone coffin of one of the Abbots of Glastonbury. A gentleman had lately broken it in two pieces. It was rotten and worm-eaten and had evidently been broken before in the same place for it was tied round with waxed twine. In the lodge there stood also a very ancient oaken chair with crossed legs and a Latin inscription, the typical 'Glastonbury Chair'. The Portress showed me the Holy Well, St Joseph's Well, in a dark corner of the crypt. The well was covered over with rotten boards. She also showed me growing just within the precincts of the Abbey a slip of the original Holy Thorn which used to grow on Weary All Hill and which is said to have sprung from the staff of St Joseph of Arimathea which he stuck into the ground when in his wanderings he first caught sight of Glastonbury and determined to end his journey in the Isle of Avalon.

The Portress told me that this slip of the Holy Thorn blooms every Christmas and remains in blossom a few days. The buds do not quite expand into flowers. . .

Wednesday, 11 September

Our party at Weston broke up today. I went on to Taunton to visit the Hockins, and the rest of the party went home to Langley. The Hockins came to the Taunton Station to meet me and drove me to the Ferns, their house at the Nursery Gardens. It is a pretty cottage of red sandstone with a conservatory, high-pitched roofs and sharp gables, and covered with a wealth and profusion of climbing plants and creepers, surrounded by its own beautiful lawns and ferneries and the Nursery Gardens which are delicious with high old-fashioned beech and hornbeam hedges for shelter. The ferneries are filled with rare ferns.

Many things about the house and place within and without reminded me strongly of Tullimaar.

It was Mrs Hockin's birthday today.

The children seemed to me much grown. Ernest has become a handsome boy with splendid eyes. Florence is a dear affectionate little thing and my godchild little Beatrice a darling. Ernest declared he remembered me.

An Archaeological Society was holding its meeting in Taunton and exploring the objects of interests in the surrounding country. As we passed Trull Church a number of drays were drawn up in the road and the Archaeologists were in the Church.

Some way further on we met two Antediluvian parsons in a gig, who seemed to have been thrown out and to be making a steeple chase towards Trull Church to fall in with the rest of the Archaeologists.

Francis Kilvert

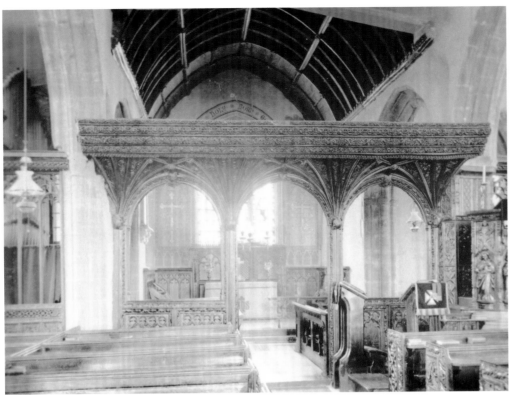

TRULL CHURCH

TAUNTON

Friday, 13 December 1872

Went to Taunton by 9.25 train.

Hockin met me at the Taunton station. It was pleasant to see dear Mrs Hockin again, looking bright and merry and like her old self. She told me about her illness. It was almost desperate at one time, and the doctors said that nothing could have saved her but her youth and a splendid constitution.

Saturday, 14 December

A gloomy wet day. The christening was at St James at a quarter to three. I baptized the child, having come down for that purpose. The child was named Lancelot Cuthbert Baines and he was wonderfully placid during the ceremony.

Mr Ford, Mr Drew and the two Miss Frys came to the christening dinner and I agreed to put off going till the midnight mail and to go up by that to be present at the dinner. Ellen Fry looked prettier than ever.

The storm of last Sunday was severely felt at Taunton. A small pinnacle over the door of St Mary's Church fell during the storm and part of it fell on the head of a young man passing at the time but his hat saved him. The tempest raged with such fury during the evening service that the sermon could scarcely be heard for the uproar and they thought the windows must be blown in. Miss Ellen Fry frightened out of her propriety and Lindley Murray exclaimed aloud ungrammatically but emphatically and with unmistakable meaning, 'I wish I hadn't came'.

Mrs Drew had indistinct notions about ferrets and asked if they were animals.

I came up by the midnight mail and reached Langley at 2.30 a.m. When I came in I found a fire in my bedroom, the kettle singing on the hob, and a strange but comfortable armchair, and sandwiches, sherry and sugar on the table.

Francis Kilvert

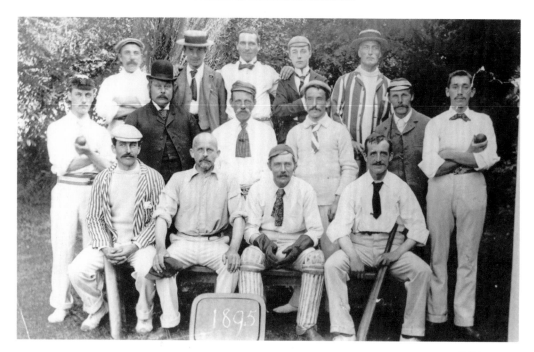

WEDMORE

CRICKET

The Cricket Club held its Annual Meeting in the Town Hall, on January 9th. Mr J.G. Knight presided over a small attendance of members. The treasurer produced a most satisfactory balance sheet, which was after inspection adopted and passed. The Secretary read the Annual Report which was considered highly satisfactory, the past season being one of the most successful the Club has ever had. Votes of thanks were given to the Treasurer and Secretary for their past services. It was decided to run an A (or Thursday) team in addition to the ordinary 1st and 2nd XI. It was resolved to start practice on Thursday, April 9th, and a resolution was passed instructing the committee to make arrangements for additional practice. (The committee have since met and decided to have an extra practice night on Wednesdays, and that a new system of practice be drafted at an early date). A hearty vote of thanks was accorded Mr Arthur Thring for the very liberal and kind way in which he supported the club during the past year. The number of members at present belonging to the club is 91, an increase of 20 on last year. The following Officers were elected for the year ending December 31st, 1896:

Patrons: (Past Presidents) H. Hobhouse, Esq., MP, R. Corner, Esq.

President, 1896: J. Huntley Thring, Esq.

Captain, 1st XI: J.S. Donne, Esq.

Sub-Captain, 1st XI: Mr W. B. Mackie.

Captain, 2nd XI: Mr E.G. Rance,

Sub-Captain, 2nd XI: Mr T. S. Donne.

Hon. Treasurer: Mr W. B. Mackie.

Hon. Secretary: Mr W. S. Donne.

General Committee: Messrs J.G. Knight, C.F. Ellerton, J. Mackie, W. R. Orledge, H.C. Pitman, E. W. Hill, J.M. Green.

Match Committee: Captain, Sub-Captain 1st XI, Secretary, and Messrs J.G. Knight, John Mackie, and C.E Ellerton.

Trustees: H. Hobhouse, Esq., MP, J.S. Donne, Esq., J. Huntley Thring, Esq.

W. S. DONNE

Castle Cary Visitor

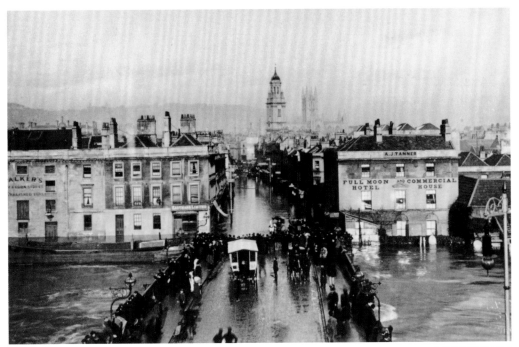

BATH FLOODS

FLOODING

Autumn crept upon us slowly this year, but it came at last, casting over nature a mantle of deepening red and golden brown, almost Canadian in the richness of its varied hues. There is no sadness in a decay so beautiful as this; the mind perceives without a teacher that these are only the signs of nature's preparation for a long slumber, and the rustling leaves whisper, as they toss before the wind, a promise of re-awaking. As I passed on my way to Bathford I enjoyed to the full the manifold beauties of this autumn scene; here a solitary tree turned to an orange brown from crown to trunk, there a fine range of chestnuts, of which one retains its native green, and the next is completely yellow, making an alternated grove; everywhere

> The fading, many coloured woods
> Shade deepening over shade, the country round
> Imbrown; a crowded umbrage, dark and dim,
> Of every hue, from wan declining green
> To sooty dark.

But another and a rarer feature was added to the landscape on this particular Sunday—'the floods were out,' and though the phrase does not carry the terror and danger to our valley that it does to other closer pent neighbourhoods, yet all the meads were covered with water and the proper current of the river was only marked by a swirling rapid in the midst of a broad lake. As you passed along the road you looked down between the houses on the water rippling up to them till you imagined you were on the seashore, and in Batheaston it had swept up to the boundary wall of the footpath, and threatened to submerge the roadway itself. The prospect of the valley from Bathford hill was therefore picturesque and striking in the extreme, as looking away towards Bath you saw the broad meadows transformed into lagoons, out of which the trees stood up like islets in the lake. Perhaps the crowning effect was imparted when, just as I was turning off by the lane to the church, a train dashed along the railway embankment which, with the flooded fields behind, seemed to be running along the shore of an American lake.

Church Rambler

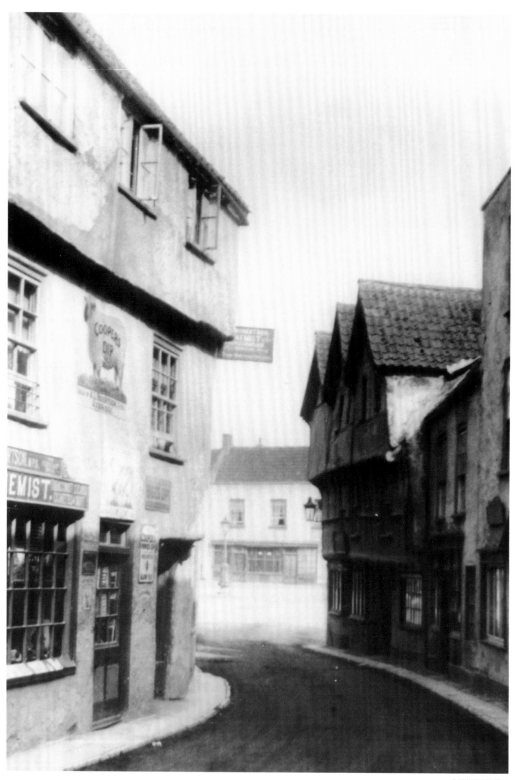

AXBRIDGE

PARADISE

It is not very far from the place where the old palace used to stand; but that has been gone a long while. You can get into Paradise from the high road by turning down a grassy lane; but the best way is to follow the brook for a little, and then go through a certain steep meadow crossed by a quavering foot-track that appears to lead straight into a hedge, and then disclaim further responsibility with the traveller. But that is only make-believe, for there is really a moss-grown, tottering stile hiding between two thorn-bushes. You must get over with caution, because on the further side the ditch is spanned by an infirm green plank; but when you are safe past that there is no more trouble about the way, for the two little paths that pretend to twist right and left really take you the same way, and that is into Paradise.

It is only a lane; but then Somerset lanes have possibilities that are far to seek in the thoroughfares of more progressive districts. If you want to know Somerset you do not keep to the turnpike road. When you wander across country among the fields of the Mendips, you are continually coming upon hamlets hidden in corners of the hills. They have an unreclaimed air, as if History had mislaid them here some centuries ago, and forgotten about them ever since. These places are full of memories and the sentiment of things gone by. The past seems to have a personality here, like a cheerful ghost basking in the sunshine, waiting until the workaday world shall slip out of being and become part of it; but it is a benevolent ghost, and does not try to play the bogey. Round about these hamlets there are many ancient roadways, disused and forgotten now, since they once belonged to conditions long dead and passed away. The original purpose of roads was to lead from homestead to homestead, and now that many of the old homesteads have dropped out of being, you can still trace the ways of past generations in the deserted lanes that you stray into by chance, and that lead you from nowhere in particular to some place 'familiar with forgotten years,' like the lane that begins in a field and leads you into the neighbourhood of a fine Elizabethan manor, now a farmhouse, standing up solitary on a green mound above green pastures on the site where, earlier still, King John had a hunting lodge. It is so still and so lonely that you almost wonder how you fail to meet an archer there.

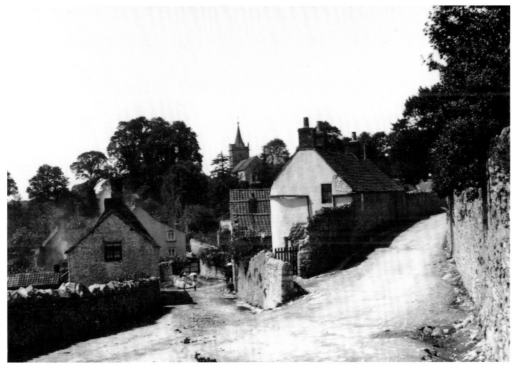

WORLE

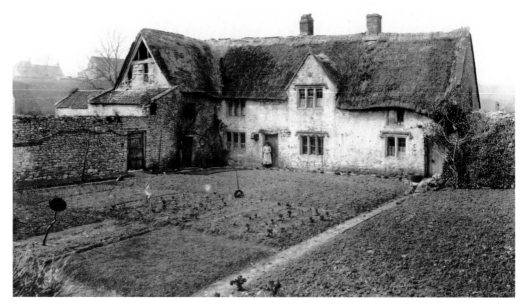

SHEPTON MALLET

But Longthorn Lane is some way from Paradise, which latter brings you near the Druid circle. It is a narrow red lane deep-sunk between high banks and great hazel-bushes that meet overhead in Midsummer, and cover the warm red earth at noon with a beautiful dappling pattern of dancing sunlight. It flickers continually with the light movement of the hazel-leaves and bewilders the eyes with its changeful lights, for the sunshine is fairly imprisoned in this narrow space, because the path rises in a long slope, and disappears suddenly at a bend, so that it seems to run away and end itself among the fugitive green shadows of the hedge. It is wonderfully silent, and the sunshine dances as if all the life of the world had slipped away and become light embodied in this still place.

Near the beginning of Paradise there is a small house with a garden round it, but the walls are broken now, and the garden has run wild with willow and thistles and broad-leaved burdock. This is the Kennels, and the hounds used to be kept here. The lane is broader and the hedge lower than it is farther on, and there is a long stretch of elder full of blossom filling the air with its heavy scent. Elder and may-blossom look like enchantment, with their wide, close expanse of flat-lying blossom that might hide things spellbound. Perhaps it was the close, heavy scent of the elder-flower that made a whistling bird on the other side of the hedge sound mysterious, but when the two of us turned back from the deserted house to pass the stretch of pale blossoms it was like the effort of grasping something in a dream, that half awakens the dreamer as the desire grows.

How the thing whistled! It was like a blackbird, but with the spiritual quality of flute-music, that seems as if the instruments were drawing the notes through its small reed-compass straight out of another world, so that the sense grasps the music but can never reach the beginning of it. And it was not quite the lyric passion of song incarnate that is the bird-carol, for there was a quiver of something like human pathos in it, a sober gaiety, like a thing delivered from peril, which, remembering pain passed by, rejoices in the fulfilment of peace. There was a long whistle, and a trill, and a few quick notes, then a soft gurgling interval, as if the piper fingered the stops very gently, and then came the long, flute-like whistle again. You could not guess where the happy thing might be hidden, for the sound seemed to come through the elder-trees; but when you came close it was just as far away as ever, and yet never very far, and always on the sunny side of the hedge. Nothing was to be seen inside the hedge but the cool green shade of the great branches; beyond was a wide meadow full of loneliness and sunshine. Still the piping went on. The Brown Brother wagged his stump of a tail and looked well pleased, but he could not say where the voice came from. So we went along the lane towards the rising part where the leaves meet overhead, and when we had got into the dappled sun-shadows the piping stopped.

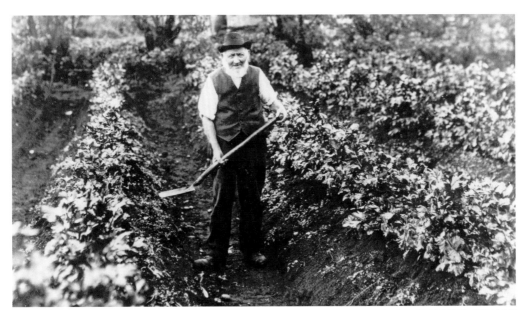

GREAT GRAMPY STEVENS, CELERY KING, WEARE

Paradise is an unfrequented place because it is too narrow for carts to pass. Nobody who goes through Paradise ever has any business there. So we went along all alone until the banks of hazel ended and the path rose up again to the level of the fields, and at the end of the bushes we met a very old man. He was walking feebly, as if all his years were a burden lying on his bent shoulders: an old, old figure in a shabby coat, leaning on a bent old stick, and bowed together with age and weakness. He looked very like one of the gnarled green pollards in the hedge that have got twisted out of shape by the West wind. When he looked round and saw the pair of us he smiled, and then he stopped and smiled again, and his old face seemed to disappear for a moment beneath a network of innumerable wrinkles. The Brown Brother, who has no manners, jumped up and pawed him, and had to be apologised for; but the old man patted his brown head and smiled again. 'You'm come droo paradise, zimly,' said he. 'A many dogs there wer' back along to wold times when I did used to bide there. Wold volks an' wold pleäces, they don't return no mwore for all the sad hearts that do mind their passin'. But there'm things what don't niver pass and them that's a-gone can mind.'—'Who lived in the old house?' the Brown Brother's companion asked him.—'Dogs,' said he, 'hounds and th' huntsman, old Ben Weaver an' his lame maiden wi' her feäce like a vlower. All dead and gone now they be, wi' their jays an' their pains—nay, what do I say, there'm jays what don't niver pass by.' He blinked his weary old eyes while he went on fondling the dog. 'Birds do zing there,' said he, 'rare an' sweet. I do mind when Ben's maid did meäke tunes so sweet's a bird wi' her little reedy-pipe. There were niver such a maid for gladness as Ben's lame maiden.' He went on talking as if he dreamed. 'All the creeturs o' the e'th, her did love so's if her'd a' had share i' the meäkin' o' them. Not a dog o' th' pack but did go crazy vur to be vondled o' she. And another there wer' volks did say wer' nigh crazy vur to wed wi' the maid, niver so lame as her were. Raison zure, vur her wer' witty beyond most, as them oft be what's afflicted. An' to hear un whistle i' the zunshine wi' her little pipe, as tho' her wer' a very bird!. . . But he wer' son to a great leädy, and couldn't a' zet by his greatness vur Ben's lame maiden. They'm dead now, all dead an' gone.'—'Did she die because of that?'—'Nay,' said the old man; 'I don't think. Why should maids die because men be vond? Her did die, and they'm all dead since, nigh fowerty year a-gone. But if zo be as the dead can mind past gladness, they'd come back zure to rejoice vur sorrow passed over. Such a maid for jay niver wer' o' this e'th; too much jay I do reckon vur that her could endure our burdens, vur they'm zore when we do grow wold. 'Twill be the better vur I when the Lard do take I, but do zim He'm not ready yet. Happen them that know did take the maid before her could vind the burden o't. But I do think when I do hear the birds a-pipen' that glad hearts gone must see their past jays an' be all the gladder vur the pain passed by and gone.'

H. Hay Wilson

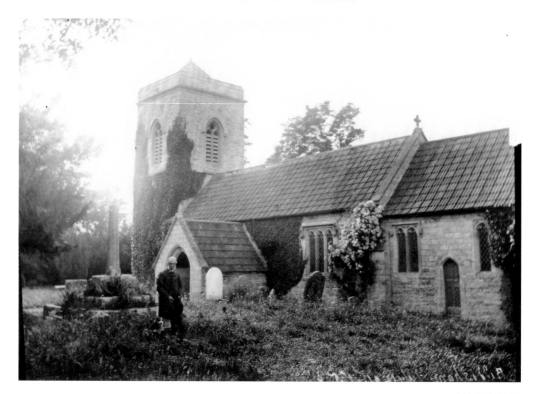

BIDDISHAM

RADSTOCK CHURCH

Though the town is in just the inchoate condition which is to be expected from its history, I was I confess surprised to find the church also infected by the grimness of the atmosphere and sharing in the ugliness of the rest of the buildings. We might have hoped to see the little church which we know once existed here, but churchwardens and the Church Building Society have been at work and we have a building with not a single stone, except perhaps part of the porch, of the slightest degree of interest. It is known that there was a church here in Norman times, and its form was preserved in the present building until the lateral extension of the nave about thirty years since. Anything more unholy than the present arrangement and state of the church it has not been my lot to see. The tower was originally a Perpendicular one, but its west window has been cut away and replaced by one of the blunt-headed windows which preceded the Gothic revival. Then about forty years ago the north wall of the nave was taken away and the church enlarged—I cannot say a north aisle was built—so that now the nave is a square chamber, in one corner of which is the chancel arch. Instead of an arcade in the nave there are a series of square wooden props, painted in imitation of oak, which are bolted to the roof as in the machine room of a factory through the flat plaster ceiling which covers all above. The likeness to a factory is increased by the square gallery which extends round two sides, and the broad flight of stairs which leads up to it from the floor of the nave. The walls too have been coloured down but the coat sadly wants renewing. The chancel was rebuilt in the last century in very bad taste and is invisible to half the people in the church. It has no east window, but over the table is a representation of the Last Supper, in a style distinctly suggestive of scene painting and nothing more. It would be well therefore if it were removed.

In passing from the structure of the church to its furniture we go from bad to worse. The high square pews face various ways and were made by someone who expected the congregation neither to have Prayer Books nor to kneel at any part of the service. There is no ledge or place for one's book, there is no kneeling-stool, nor is there room between the broad seat and the front of the pew to kneel on the floor without great difficulty. What is worse the pew in which I was placed was offensively dirty. The heating pipes are laid above the floor, though no doubt the expense of excavating has been saved in the hope of rebuilding. But the doors are numbered with

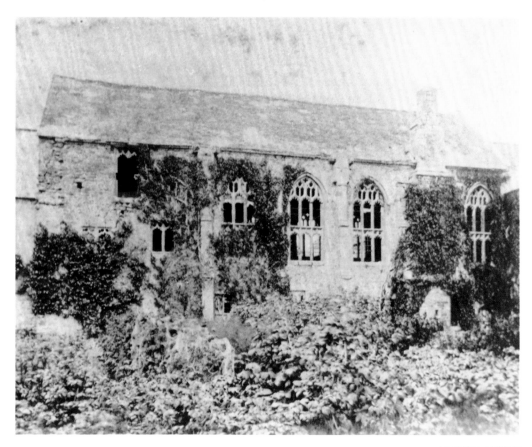

CLEEVE ABBEY

large printed labels such as we see on the pens at cattle shows. The nave is chiefly lighted by two windows, one of which rises above the other to match the precipitous piling up of the clerk's desk, reading-desk and pulpit beside it. When the minister reached the top and stood behind the faded velvet cushions of the pulpit an impassable barrier seemed placed between him and the congregation. I pity the speaker or preacher who strives at such a distance, great in reality and greater in effect, to bring the minds of his hearers into sympathy with his own, and to make their hearts responsive to his teaching.

The oldest part of the church is the south wall, and attached to this is the porch in which is a stone with an interesting sculpture of the crucifixion, and another with two figures. But even here the hand of desecration has been. A public gas lamp is fixed to the exterior, and the supply pipe for this is carried carelessly through the porch from the church in a fashion scarcely tolerated in a blind alley.

Church Rambler

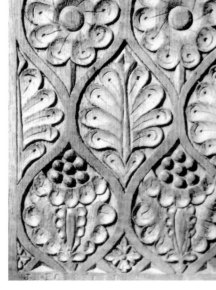

FROM A CARVING CLASS, LOCKING

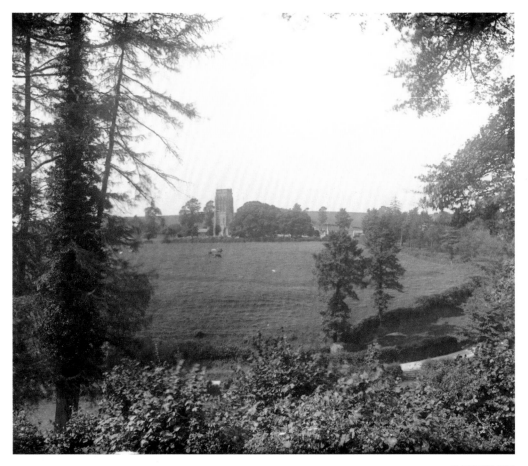

BATCOMBE

LULLINGTON

Lullington has almost the appearance of a model village. Not, that is to say, of a new-fangled cluster of houses—the whim of a noble-minded but inexperienced philanthropist—which seems from the staring bran-newness which it opposes to the varied tints of fields and trees, and hills and sky around it and above it, as if it were hated by Nature: a thing that has not yet learned to obey her laws, and to accept the conditions under which alone she will throw over the habitations of men a corner of her mantle of beauty and put them in harmony with herself. On the contrary the little homes of Lullington have formed part of this pretty landscape for a period far beyond legal memory, and studious care has manifestly been taken that it shall enjoy the full benefit of this advantage and appear in every respect an old English village. Beyond the church there is really no building worthy of particular notice, yet in the general appearance of the village there is an indefinite charm which strongly impresses the visitor, as he suddenly comes upon it from a country lane which diverges from the main road to Frome, and shows him Wolverton Church on his right hand as he passes along, and Road and the ugly spirelets of Road hill on his left. The population of Lullington is a purely agricultural one and only numbers about one hundred and fifty souls. There is no great house in the parish, but it is the property of the owner of the adjoining parish of Orchardley, and it is to the house there that the people look for their head.

Church Rambler

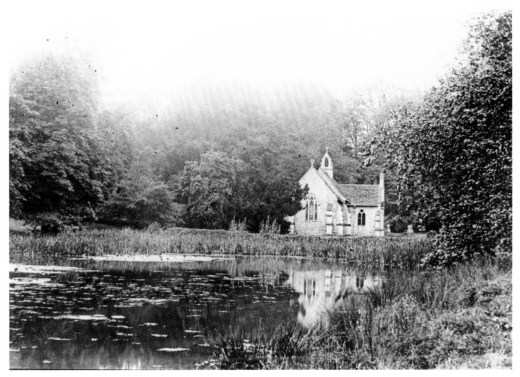

ORCHARDLEIGH CHURCH

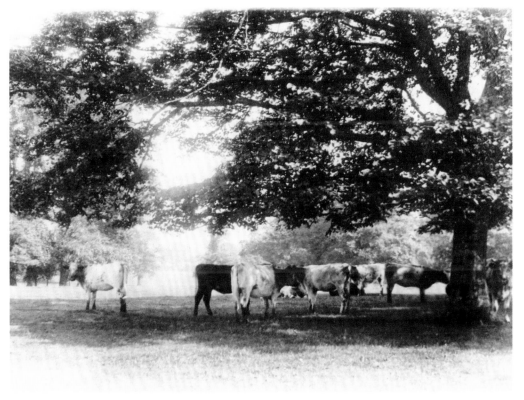

ORCHARDLEIGH PARK

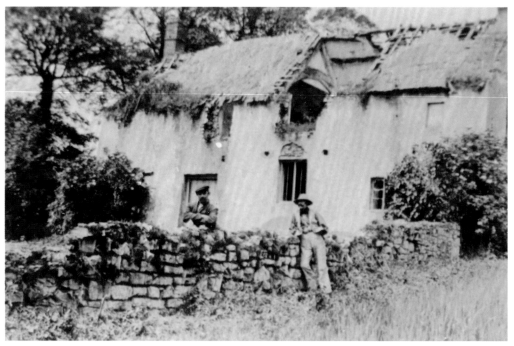

IDSTOCK

RURAL POVERTY

I ascertained that in this neighbourhood wages had received some kind of addition just previous to my visit, and that for the most skilled work they were 11s. or 12s. a week. I was little prepared, however, for what I saw a few miles farther on the road, in the parish of Banwell, and about six miles from Weston-super-Mare. Lying a little way back from the road, I descried what I should have thought was a pigstye, but for the fact that a man was at a kind of door, cutting up a dead sheep. I called him out and questioned him concerning himself and his cottage. I was then invited by him to visit the interior of the latter. Unless I had seen it I could not have believed that such a place could exist in England. I had to stoop very low to get inside this habitation of an English agricultural labourer. The total length of the miserable hut was about seven yards, its width three yards, and its height, measured to the extreme point of the thatched roof, about ten feet; the height of the walls, however, not being so much as six feet. From the top of the walls was carried up to a point the thatched roof, there being no transverse beams or planks. In fact, had there been any, I could not have stood upright in this hovel. There was, of course, no second floor to the place, and the one tiny floor was divided in the middle into two compartments, each being about three yards square; one used for a bedroom and the other for a sitting-room. The ground was irregularly paved with large stones, with earth between and in their crevices. On my remarking that the floor must be very damp, if not wet, in winter, the man said, 'Oh, no, sir, it don't "heave" much;' by which he meant that the moisture did not come up very much through the stones. From the thatch, in all directions, hung festoons of spiders' webs, intermingled with sprays of ivy, which, but for the terrible squalor of the place, would have given a romantic appearance to the hut.

John P— (the inhabitant of this 'cottage') was a short, thickset man sixty years of age. He had lived there, he told me, a quarter of a century. His predecessors were a man, his wife, and six children, all of whom he said had slept in the 'bedroom,' nine feet square. John told me that he could not work now so well as he used to do; but nevertheless he looked strong and healthy for his age; and his principal duty—a responsible one—was to look after his master's stock. His wages were 5s. a week. Out of that he paid his master £2 10s. a year rent for his 'cottage,' and 10s. a year more for the privilege of running his pig—for John had a pig, as well as some fowls—on his master's land. John also rented one-eighth of an acre of potato ground, for which—still out of his miserable wages—he paid 15s. a year. And yet this man was happy amidst it all. His

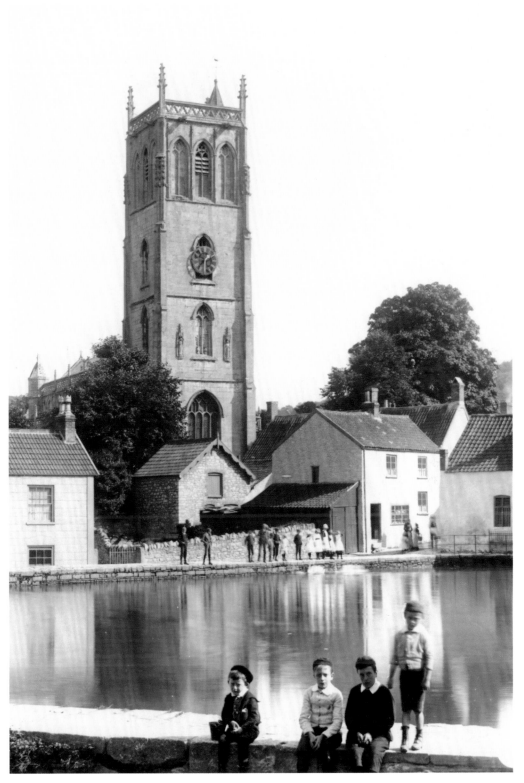

BANWELL

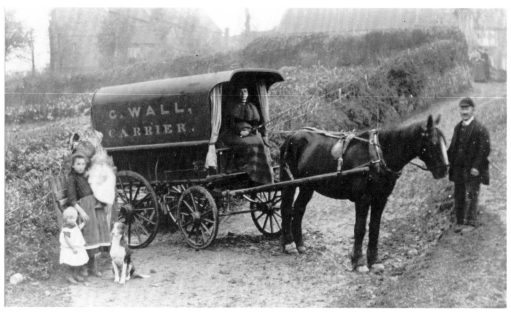

LADY CARRIER, STOKE SUB HAMDON

wretched patched garments looked singularly inconsistent when viewed in connexion with his happy-looking face. He spoke well of his employer. His cottage walls were made of hardened mud, and some time since the rain had come through the old thatched roof, and he thought it was very good of his master to put a new roof and a new door to his 'cottage' when he asked him to do so. John had been married, but had lost his wife. One daughter, however, was still living, and she had married a policeman in London. John said that when his cottage became no longer fit—according to John's idea of fitness—for a 'residence,' 'the master' intended to throw down the mud walls and plough up the site.

F. G. Heath

HOPE FOR THE LABOURERS

Somersetshire is one of the largest counties in England, comprising an area of 1,642 square miles, or to speak agriculturally, 1,050,880 acres; and it is a singular circumstance that, being naturally one of the richest of the English counties, the status of its rural labourers should be so low. From the observations which I have made I have come to the conclusion that it is, as a rule, in those parts of the country where the condition of the agricultural labourers is the most miserable and wretched, that there exists the least desire on the part of that truly unfortunate class to raise themselves from their abject position. . .

Notwithstanding the general indifference of the Somersetshire agricultural labourers to their wretched condition, I was glad to find no lack in that county of those philanthropic efforts which alone will conduce to the real elevation of the rural labourer. The truly noble work which Canon Girdlestone carried on in Devonshire for so many years, I found had commenced in Somersetshire, and the man who is fairly entitled to the credit of having originated the movement is my friend Mr Robert Arthur Kinglake, a brother of 'Eothen,' who is also known to fame as the historian of the Crimean war. On the occasion of an annual visitation of Archdeacon Denison to his clergy, which took place at Taunton on the 15th April in the present year, there was a dinner given, at which the archdeacon, the clergy of the deanery, and a large number of the county gentlemen and farmers were present. Mr Kinglake, in an after dinner speech proposed 'Prosperity to the Yeomanry of Somerset!' and whilst congratulating the farmers present on their general prosperity and the progress they had made in education, took the opportunity of referring to the deplorable condition of the agricultural labourers in the county. That was the first occasion of any real prominence being given to the

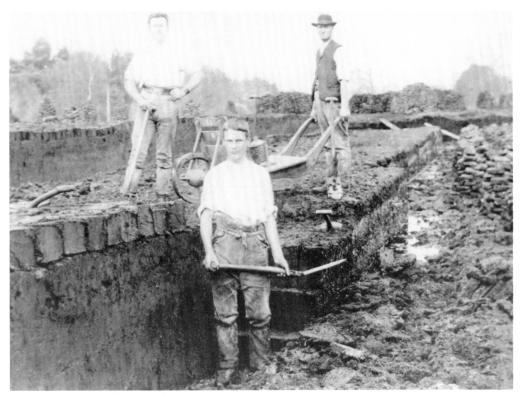

TURF CUTTERS

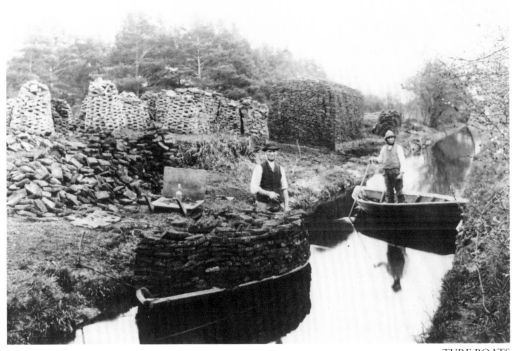

TURF BOATS

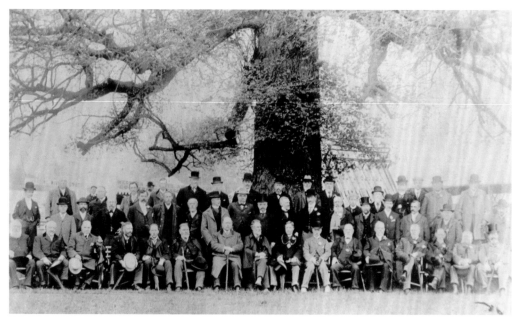

AGRICULTURAL SHOW, TAUNTON

subject of the labourer in Somersetshire since the commencement of the Warwickshire 'strike;' and it required no small courage in an assemblage of landed proprietors, farmers, and divines—the latter of whom do not generally, I am sorry to say, take that active interest which they might do in the cause of the labourer—to speak out boldly for the poor peasants.

The feeling of the agriculturists at the meeting was manifested by very impatient exclamations during the delivery of the excellent remarks which were made by Mr Kinglake. He is a county magistrate of twenty years' standing, and being one who professes old Whig or modern Liberal-Conservative principles, it cannot be said that his advocacy of the cause of the labourers is the result of that ultra-Radical or revolutionary tendency which is alleged to have given rise to the agricultural labourers' movement. Mr Kinglake said that he was glad there were no agricultural 'strikes' in Somersetshire, but he much regretted to find that wages were so low as 8s. and 9s. a week in many parishes, especially in the neighbourhood of Wellington, Stoke-St-Gregory, and Long Sutton. Three suggestions which were made by Mr Kinglake are so excellent that they deserve particular notice. The first was that the system should be adopted in England which has for some time been the practice in Scotland, namely, that a register of farm labourers should be kept in agricultural towns in the same way as registers are now kept for domestic servants. The second suggestion was that societies should be formed all over the country for repairing and building labourers' cottages: such societies had already been formed in Kent, Shropshire, and other counties, and had proved successful. The third suggestion, which Mr Kinglake originated, is one admirably calculated to advance the cause of the rural labourer. It was that a weekly journal should be started especially devoted to the interests of the farm labourers. This is an excellent idea, and as almost every class in the country has now its organ, it is to be hoped that some philanthropic individual may be induced to start what might be called the Agricultural Labourers' Journal. I am firmly convinced that the agricultural labourers' movement will never be put down until their present deplorable condition is ameliorated. There are many noble hearts in this country ready and willing to come to the assistance of this downtrodden race of men. But London readers can have but little idea of the great difficulty of the undertaking in remote rural districts. Noble and disinterested efforts are being made by such men as Canon Girdlestone and Mr Arthur Kinglake, but they have a hard battle to fight against the landed proprietors and the farmers, whose active enmity they have in many instances to encounter.

F. G. Heath

THE LABOURING POOR

On entering Montacute I was forcibly struck by the loveliness of the scenery immediately surrounding the village. The first object of note is the splendid mansion of the Phelips family, who are the great land owners in the district, the whole of Montacute, I believe, and some of the land in the adjoining villages belonging to them. The wages I found had recently been augmented in consequence of the 'strike' of the agricultural labourers in different parts of the country, and were then 10s. a week—on the average possibly a little less. Only a short time previously, however, they were 9s. a week. I made a great number of inquiries in the houses of the poor labourers, and I elicited the most painful facts. It was impossible for me to see such scenes of wretchedness without feeling compelled to tender some relief before quitting the miserable hovels.

In all the cases which I have enumerated cider was given, generally three pints, but sometimes only two pints daily, reckoned at 1d. per pint, or in the case of an allowance of three pints per day, 1s. 6d. per week. In some cottages which I visited the rooms were almost bare of furniture. The single bedrooms, which in many cases had to accommodate the whole of a family, often contained nothing but a squalid bedstead, and perhaps a small table and a broken chair, with a few ragged clothes on the bedsteads, not nearly enough to keep the poor creatures warm. Clothes, in fact, which would have been barely sufficient to cover one bed, had to serve also for the covering of the little ones who had to lie about in different parts of the floor.

Amidst all this terrible poverty of the peasants in Montacute, the land in the neighbourhood is some of the richest in the whole of the county. In fact, its productiveness is so extraordinary that I was assured by a competent authority that a large farmer could realise a fortune in seven years in the district. The farmers there pay 1*l*. 10s. and 2*l*. an acre for land that is worth 4*l*. and 5*l*. an acre respectively, and the profits on farming are consequently enormous. One farm contains 500 acres of land worth about 4*l*. an acre but for which the farmer pays about 30s. an acre. On this farm I found that ten men only were employed, and on another farm of 200 acres that two men only were employed. There are in Montacute three other farms, containing respectively 240, 144, and 134 acres.

I was informed on the most reliable authority that one piece of ground in the parish, consisting of eight acres, had in eighteen months produced three crops—two of clover, and one of wheat. The value of each entire crop of clover was 45*l*., and the value of the wheat crop was at the rate of 14*l*. an acre. Yet for this very land, so enormously productive, only 2*l*. 5s. an acre was paid as rent.

F. G. Heath

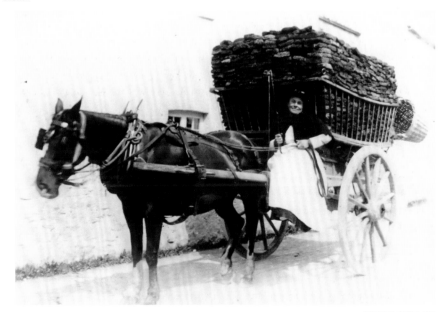

TURF SELLER

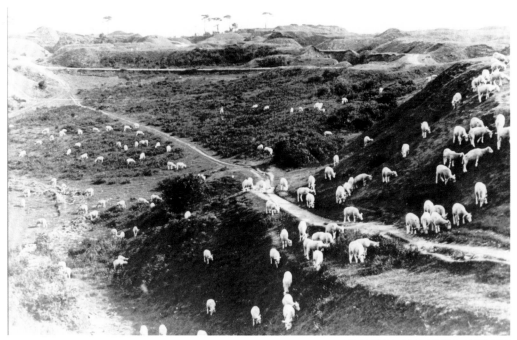

GRAZING, HAM HILL QUARRY

THE SHEPHERD ON THE HILLS

March had come in like a lion, as it should do traditionally, and it was still early in the month when I was caught in a veritable blizzard of snow, with a biting north wind, and had to take shelter. I shared it with Silas Noldart, the shepherd, an old friend of mine, whom I found cutting bread and cheese upon his knee as he crouched under the lee of a thatched hurdle on the downs.

Silas is seventy, hard and gnarled as a pollard oak, with a mass of white hair and a venerable beard flowing down his smock. He pulled his forelock, by way of obeisance, as I paused for a breather and snuggled down beside him. A glorious panorama of hill and dale was spread out at our feet, and in the bright intervals between the storms we could see forty miles away to the west.

'Your lambs play as if they enjoyed this weather, Noldart,' I began.

'Aye, I likes to see 'em lep about,' he replied, "tis a sign of 'ealth. We done the same in our day, sir, I doubt; but they'm a-thought more lordly wi' the yeos at meal times nor we was. Fruzzling their tails is their way o' asking a blessing from the only God they knows—mother.'

'Yes; it's a fine sheep-running down round about here.'

'Aye—well favoured for the she'p. They do lep, don't 'em? Catched it from this country they'm bred in, likely. When Israel come to take him a change o' pasture out o' Egypt, this 'ere country was young, I doubt, and overreached itself capering and skipping in honour of the festival, I reckon; and by a shift o' the wind or some'at, got left in 'ills and 'ummocks afore they could on-stretch theirselves.'

'You read your psalms then, Noldart?'

'Can't read a word, sir—but I've 'eard 'em say about it. Wonnerful human things is she'p, or I suppose, as they was made fust, we should say wonnerful she'ply things is humans. "Gone astray like a she'p," we say: they fangles through the 'edges and gets a brimble in their trousers, and calls for the shepherd to pick it out and take 'em back again. 'Tis the same wi' we, ain't it?'

'And where do you go to church, Noldart?'

'Church going or chapel going is on-possible, sir, for I. We'm all a sweet smelling savour, and coming afore Him He'll know our trade by the smell o' we and say: "You'm a shepherd, chapel be excused; I got another flock for you 'ere: 'tis what I fitted you for, so o' course you'm fit for nothing else—take on this lot."

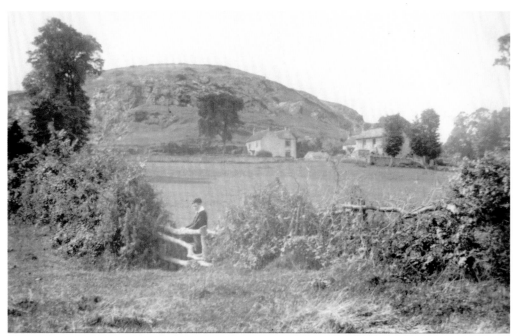

RUSTIC STILE

'Then there's the lost she'p: how the yeo fusses about it for a time—doesn't know where 'tis to, and no use for me to explain as 'tis all right, and we knows. 'Tis so with ours and God, if we'd only be content: He can't explain, and we shouldn't be understanding if He did:

Alfred Percivall

THE SHEPHERD'S LOST LOVE

'Yes—they'm silly things comparisoned to dogs is the she'p, and therefore want more understanding than most: needs a lot o' patience to master their folly. And they gets sillier as they gets older, is my opinion. A lamb seems more senseful than a yeo—can at least play: when 'e's dropped that 'e's dropped all the sense 'e got seemingly. 'Tis the same with wummin, you know'

'Oh! that is your experience as a married man, is it, Noldart?'

I never was married, sir: needed all me powers for the she'p. I never could abear to argufy with no one: I don't need to wi' she'p, I sends Beller. I'm wishing time and again, now I be middle-aged, as I 'ad took a wumman, but I give all me time to Farmer Trepplin, and 'ave worked on this farm for 'is father and 'im fifty-two year last Christmas. I told 'im so a month agone, and asked if 'e could allow me a trifle to give up: but 'e says "No"—very close-woven man is Farmer Trepplin, real West of England cloth 'e is—and I must give up my cottage, 'e says, if I leave. That I couldn't, seeing as I 'ave lived in 'er forty year, and lodged in 'er ten afore that.

'I near married once though—I'm not telling you who with 'cause you knows 'er: "go and touch" that was, as they say, but we 'ad a fall out just in time—argufying as usual. She asked me to go for a walk with 'er one evening, and I called to fetch 'er.

"'Better take a numbriller, 'tis going to rain," I says.

"'No, it ain't," she say, "and I shan't."

"'Ave it your own way," I says.

"'No, I won't," she say.

"'We'll wait and see then," I says.

"'No, we won't," she say: "it ain't going to rain."

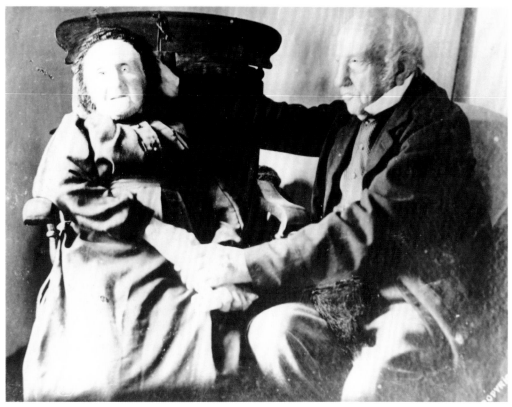

OLD AGE

'So I just stands and looks at her without a word.

"'Can't yer say something or do something?" she went on. "I say it ain't going to rain; now then?"

"'Well," I says, "you won't 'ave it my way, nor yet your own way, nor even wait and see the Lord's way: what is there for I to say or do?"

"'Bunches!" she say, "and if you can't say something or do something we shan't suit."

"'Very well," I says, and leaves 'er door, and goes off home. 'There you might suppose was the end, but not a bit of it. Ten minutes later she come down to my door, and 'twas raining then: and she say, "You was wrong: 'twas not going to rain when you said 'twas: it comed on after."

"''Tis what I meant," I says.

"'No, you never," she say: "and 'tis not what I call rain even now—'tis but a smizzle. You say, "Tis going to rain': you never say when, or for 'ow long, or 'ow 'ard and that"—you never say nothing. If you'd a' said 'twill be going to rain, 'twould ha' been some sense to it. But you say, ''Tis going to rain,' and 'twasn't going to rain when you spoke it, and didn't rain for long after: and it ain't what I call rain now: 'tis but a smizzle. And you say, 'Better take a numbriller'; now a numbriller is for rain, and this be only a smizzle. There be rain and rain, same as there is men and men; but there aren't numbrillers and numbrillers, but just a numbriller; and a numbriller isn't for a smizzle, and you say 'take a numbriller'—where's the sense in a numbriller for a smizzle? Drat the man! If you can't say something or do something, you won't suit–"'

"'Sam," I says (that was my dog at that day)—"Sam, thiefs!" That cleared 'er, though Sam wasn't really in the 'ouse at all, being on duty in the she'p-fold. That was the end. If you go courting, seems to me you 'm courting all sorts of things you'm not wanting.'

Alfred Percivall

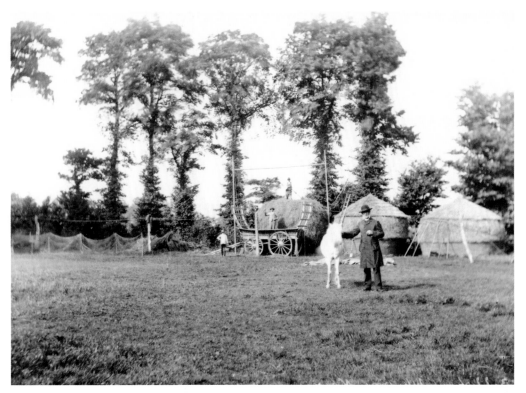

BIDDISHAM

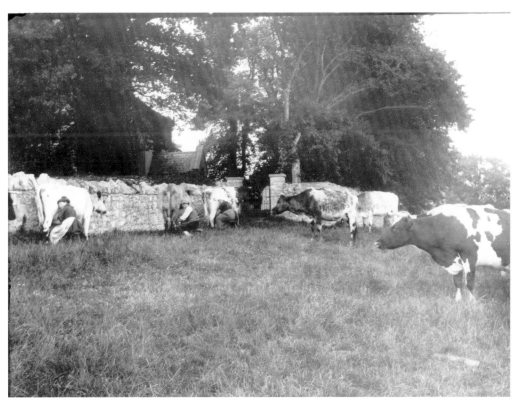

MILKING, BIDDISHAM

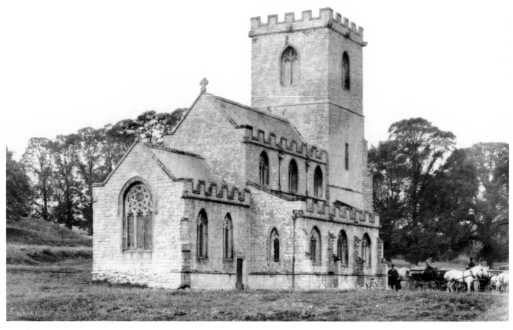

LOW HAM CHURCH

DIARY OF THE REVD S.O. BAKER, VICAR OF MUCHELNEY AND LOW HAM

1880

January	A very cold and severe winter. Very good skating on Langport Moor.
	School Committee outvoted the Vicar as to the use of the Schoolroom for parish dances.
May	Unhealthy spring, much illness. Throat complaints. No sheep in the Parish.
June	Wet haymaking and poor crop. Reduction 10 per cent.
August	A month of hot, dry, weather, good harvest and well got in. All wheat and corn in by the end of Month. Scarcely any Apples or wall fruit. Wasps unusually abundant.
September	Choir treat, Muchelney and Low Ham; by train to Weston junction, thence in carriages to Burrington Coomb. 30 present.
	Muchelney women received into Drayton Female Club.
	Court House garden enlarged, and new drains put in to the premises.

£10 was collected in the Parish as a New Year's present to the Schoolmistress.

William Woodborne's workshop burnt in the early spring, unaccountably. Many incendiary fires round us, at Ash, Curry and Drayton. £8 collected for him.

Joseph Wood appointed Sexton at Easter 1879 in place of George Sharman, deceased.

Greatest number of Communicants this year at any one celebration, 25.

New communicants: Ann Amelia (Minnie) White

Matilda Hill White

Mrs Duckett

1895

The year began with snow. It fell heavily on Jan. 12th and the next day melted rapidly. The roads were in such a state that services were held in the Schoolroom and there was no reaching Low Ham. From the 13th to 25th water was deep on the Langport road, but on Sunday it was free. On 29th snow fell heavily. Then frost set in and continued with E and NE winds till Feb. 24th. The Low Ham salary is reduced (from Xmas) from £63 to £50 and the Patron desires a monthly Communion there, which involves the monthly

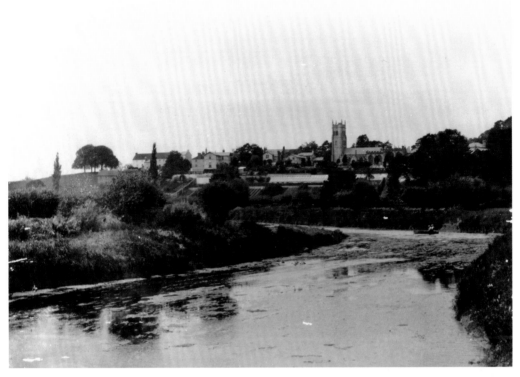

LANGPORT

procuring of a substitute at Muchelney in the morning. Mr Lutley, Rector of East Lambrook, will come at £1:3:6 each time. Very late Spring. Throughout April and May scarcely a shower and North winds continuously. The Bishop, Dr Kennion, visiting, and holding Confirmations in each parish in the Taunton Archdeaconry. At Easter it was determined to dis-continue a Church-rate and make a collection instead for Church expenses. In October a thorough cleaning and colouring and stopping inside and outside, of the Church and walls was carried out and the Chancel ceiling was coloured on the lines of Street's decoration at Yatton. An epidemic of measles in September and October, School closed for 6 weeks. Mild Christmas.

NAME THIS CHILD

As we sat and chatted thus, the snow still falling in gusts and Noldart still munching his bread and cheese, a friendly and inquisitive red-breast perched upon a hurdle in front of us, on the look out for crumbs.

'I never see one o' them things,' said my friend, pointing at it with his knife, 'but what I think of Mary Stimmer's youngest brat what was also a lost she'p. Stimmers was a carter, but 'e took 'im a bad cold one Feb'ury which put 'im out in one puff and soon after the child was borned. I'd knowed Mary from a girl, and me and Stimmers 'ad schooled together. And she say to me, "Silas, you must come and stand god-sire to the boy: I got no one now my man's gone to give an eye to 'im as 'e grows up: 'twould be neighbourly-like and that." You see, she done a bit o' mending and cooking for I, times. O' course, we chapel folk don't hold with such ceremonials as Mary did, but I says I will. 'Twas the first and only time I ever been to a church service, and the rules did seem a thought cur'ous. Minister were quite a lad, a curat, and 'e come down in a white smock to the "copper" what was fixed behind the front door.'

'We call it a font,' I explained.

'Aye, I believe I 'ave heard that afore: well, the fount, then. Fust go off Master Curat wasn't for letting my dog Sly come in, though there wasn't above four or five folk inside, and plenty of room.

'"God took and made her same as He done you, sir," I says: "and she serves Him same as you do, sir," I says: "only she'm better off in the number of legs."

'"I must put her into the porch," he say.

'"Please don't you lift a finger to her, sir," I says, "or maybe she'll fix it: 'tis a rum bitch, she is, is Sly."

'She knowed as we was discussing 'er as well as well, and I see 'er lick and curl 'er lips: so I told 'er to go and lay at the doorway. So that was settled.

'Next, Mary Stimmers must go and get "cast" in 'er seat, and couldn't get up—weak in one leg she was: so I 'ad to go and set 'er on 'er feet, and then we made a fairy-ring around the fount.

'Now she'd took and told me as we was suspected to do a bit o' back-answering with the gentleman, as we walked to the church. 'I ain't over-well up in it myself," she say, "but you'll find it all writ in the Book." But being no scholard, when the time came I left the exact wording to 'er, and just touched me 'ead and said, "Aye, aye, sir," "Same 'ere, sir," and "I'm with Mary Stimmers, sir," as was only fair, seeing the baby belonged to 'er.

'But what I really *did* take notice of was a robin redbreast what was in the church, and what spended 'is time flitting back and fro between the preacher's dock and the fount: 'e seemed to me to be bent on a mischief, or anyhow to be there for a purpose: so I watch it careful, and sure enough when the minister took the nipper into 'is arms, and say to Mary: "The name of this child?" master robin flut by and remembered 'isself right down the front of the baby's gown'd.

'Yet in face o' that Mary sings out: "'is name is 'Erbert."

'"No, pardon me on the other 'and, sir, 'is name is Robin," I says.

'Minister looks from she to I, and from I to she, and seems lost.

'"Erbert," she say again.

'"Robin," I says.

'"Erbert, an you please, sir," she say a third time, and drops a curtsey. That looked like ending of it, for the curat took and dippit 'is 'and in the copper—fount, I would say, then. So I ups quick, and took the nipper out of is arms, and Sly, seein' some'at was a'foot, paddled in and looks up in me face for orders: and as the curat looked fudgetty, "Guard 'im," I says to Sly, lest 'e might give it all up and be off. And then leading Mary apart I says: "You must ha' got a maggot in your 'ead, Mary Stimmers: he'm a lucksome bird is yon, as you

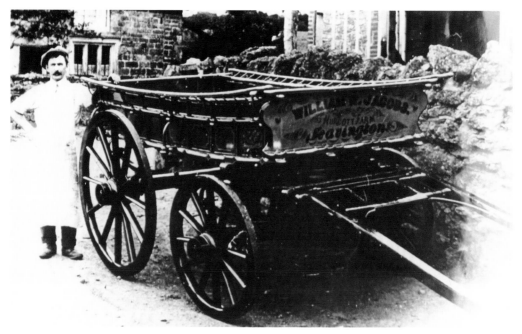

well know; and seein' as 'e was sent to mark the nipper, as 'e done, for a 'Robin,' 'tis flying in the face o' things for you to stick to "Erbert': 'tis ongainly for the future of 'im like enough, to take and cross the bird. You stick against it, and I'll 'ave nothing to do wi' the whole flummery! 'Tis my first duty as god-sire to show you your error. There's only one thing we can do as neighbours—I'll go 'alves with you: take the fore-end o' mine and the back-end o' yours and make it 'Robert,' but that be as far as I dare: you can still call 'im 'Bert' just the same you see."

'So there we settled it, and "Robert" it were: and out again went Sly.'

'At the end, the minister say we 'm to take the nipper to the bishop when 'e can talk plain, and meantime 'e was to be instructed by Church Chastism. Mary she wasn't 'tending just then, so "I'll see to it, sir," I says, "and if that don't do no good, a ash-plant and that is 'andy." But 'e wasn't listening and walked off up the church to the waiting-room. I don't know what the church done, but I did my bit, though it wasn't a morsel o' use—lost she'p 'e was. O' course wi' such a start 'e couldn't come to much good, 'twasn't to be suspected: nor Mary nor I ain't seen 'im since 'e turned eighteen (that's over thirty years back-along): must ha' been drownded in a sewer afore now, I reckon.'

Alfred Percivall

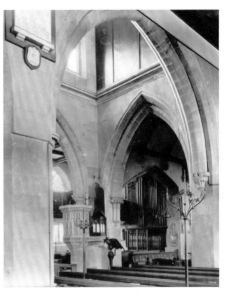

SHEPTON MALLET

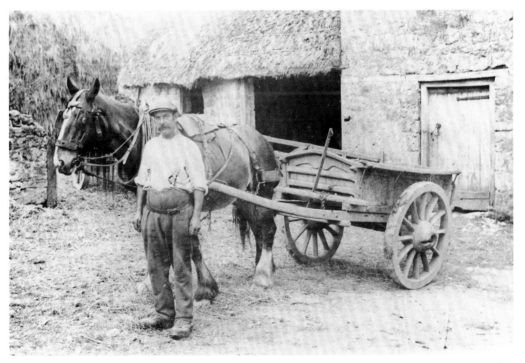

CARTER, STOKE SUB HAMDON

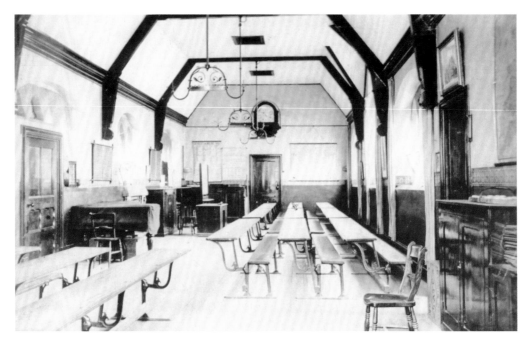

WOOKEY SCHOOL

EDUCATION

Of late one has sometimes been inclined to fear that the universal spread of education will before long efface all interesting local peculiarities, and bring the entire population to the unpicturesque level of a Board School teacher. But a few hours with these Somersetshire children effectually dispelled that dread. Never had their dialect sounded broader or more uncompromisingly provincial than when they were answering historical questions and solving arithmetical problems. The very education displayed in their answers rendered more conspicuous the form in which it was clothed. 'Plaize, zur, 'e cotched un!' exclaimed a clever little boy, anxious to give information respecting the capture of Richard Coeur de Lion; and although at a warning glance from the teacher he hurriedly substituted a more conventional rendering of the idea, it was evident that the grammar acquired during school-hours had by no means become part and parcel of his life. So generally is this fact now realised that in certain small schools, where only a very limited number of subjects are taught, grammar has been recently discarded as a worthless study; children, fresh from writing an elaborate page of parsing, relapsing straightway into the same manner of speech that has sufficed their fathers before them. After all it seems but fitting that some little individualities should linger on in a nook where the labourers play bowls of a summer's evening, and the very stones tell of an older and more picturesque age. As usual, those on the spot are least conscious of their aesthetic privileges. In the wall of an old farmhouse, that with its attendant buildings forms at least half the village, there is a curiously wrought stone mullioned window, of such unusual design and evident antiquity as instantly to catch a stranger's eye. But to the villagers it is simply the dairy-window, and nothing more.

Anon

SCHOOL INSPECTION

Having little experience of the present system of rural education, it was with some curiosity that we settled down in a corner of the schoolroom, ready to judge of the results of twelve months' instruction on the sturdy country children before us. It was very evident, from the serious demeanour of everybody concerned, that this visit of the government inspector constituted one of the most important events of the year. The young schoolmistress, a pleasant specimen of a freshlooking farmer's daughter, had worried the bloom out of her cheeks, and herself into a bad headache, before the examination began. Yet this anxiety was not, as is

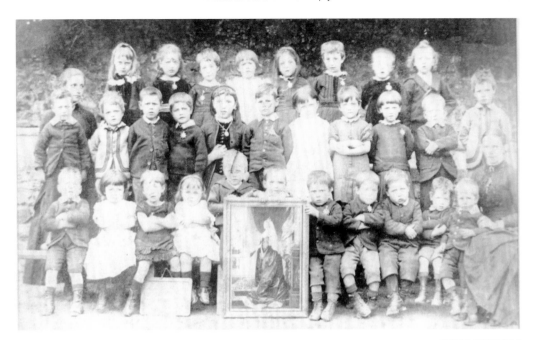

WELLINGTON

frequently the case in similar circumstances, connected with monetary considerations; for, quite independent of the results of the examination, she received a regular salary of £50 a year together with a dwelling-house and fuel. The money is partly drawn from an ancient charitable bequest for the education of certain children in the parish, the details of which are duly set forth on a large blackboard kept in the belfry, and this sum is supplemented by the government grant, the squire and rector combining to make up the deficit, if any. This has been found on the whole a better plan than allowing the salary to fluctuate according to the size of the grant. The latter course is sometimes adopted with a view to encouraging the schoolmistress to do her best, but it frequently leads to complaints of undue pressure on the children, and does not make fair allowances for incapacity or absence consequent on ill-health. . .

Sometimes of course the questions did not elicit precisely the answers that were intended, as when the inspector inquired what was known about the English Bible, a little boy replied fluently: 'It was chained in a church, and the people would bide there for several hours to hear it read all through.' But when all possible detractions are made, what an astonishing idea it is that in future the majority of young farm labourers will be able to supply one offhand with the date of the battle of Agincourt, while even the boy whose function in life is to scare crows, will be in a position to pass judgment on the conduct of William the First towards the conquered Saxons! And it is confidently hoped by those who know the agricultural labourer that, as he becomes better acquainted with the history of the vast empire to which he belongs, a feeling of national pride will gradually replace the narrow parochial prejudices by which his horizon has hitherto been bounded.

Anon

BURRINGTON SCHOOL

Situated in the Vale of Wrington, and in close proximity to the line of the Mendip Hills, is the beautiful village of Burrington. From the village of Wrington I drove to this place. By the kindness of the Vicar's family I was permitted to see the excellent school connected with Burrington church. The vicar is the Revd William Bishop de Moleyns, MA, who has earnestly laboured for twenty years in the neighbourhood. He was for the greater part of that time the curate of Wrington, but was so universally beloved by the people in all the country round that the living of Burrington was presented to him by the parishioners, in whose gift it is. . .

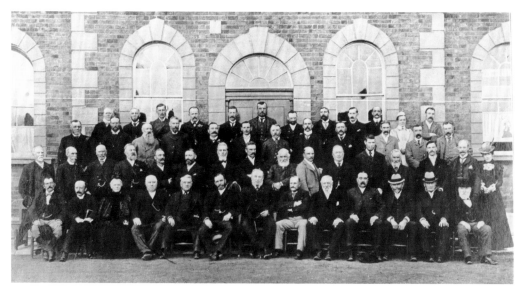

BOARD OF GUARDIANS, TAUNTON

In the midst of a population of only 400 souls he has a school of boys and girls numbering no less than 103, principally the children of the peasants, although the education, given under the immediate superintendence of the excellent master and mistress, is so good that farmers are induced to send their children to the school. During my visit to the schoolroom the children sang a simple melody, entitled Always speak the truth, and I considered that for so young a band the execution was admirable. No compulsory educational system is required at Burrington; and I think it is a remarkable circumstance that with so small a population so good and so flourishing a school should be established and maintained. A necessary enlargement of the existing school building is required, and I sincerely hope that the necessary funds will be very soon forthcoming. If one thing is required more than another to raise the peasant to his proper position in the social scale, it is efforts for the education of the children of the labouring poor such as are being so nobly put forth at Burrington by the Revd Mr de Moleyns.

Since my visit to the Burrington vicarage a dark shadow has fallen over the household of the excellent Vicar. Mrs de Moleyns, a loving wife, a tender mother, and a good and true friend to the poor in her village, is now no more. Her death was very sudden, and I felt deeply pained on hearing the sad intelligence, because I had visited the home that was made bright by her presence, and had heard of her good and gentle life. For nearly twenty years she had quietly and unostentatiously been doing the work of a truly Christian lady, and whilst her loss is bitterly felt in her own home circle, it is a loss that is scarcely less felt in the homes of the peasantry in Burrington and its neighbourhood, where, whilst her active benevolence has relieved the wants of the sick, her Christian sympathy has been ever ready to comfort the sorrowful.

F. G. Heath

DUNSTER MILL

At Dunster there is a curious mill which has two wheels, overshot, one in front of the other, and both driven by the same sluice. It was very hot as we stood by the wheels; the mill dust came forth and sprinkled the foliage so that the leaves seemed scarce able to breathe: it drifted almost to the stream hard by, where trout were watching under a cloud of midges dancing over the ripples. They look as if entangled in an inextricable maze, but if you let your eye travel, say to the right, as you would follow the flight of a bird, you find that one side of the current of insects flies up that way, and the other side returns. They go to and fro in regular order, exactly like the fashionable folk in Rotten Row, but the two ranks pass so quickly that looked at both together the vision cannot separate them, they are faster than the impression on the retina.

Richard Jefferies

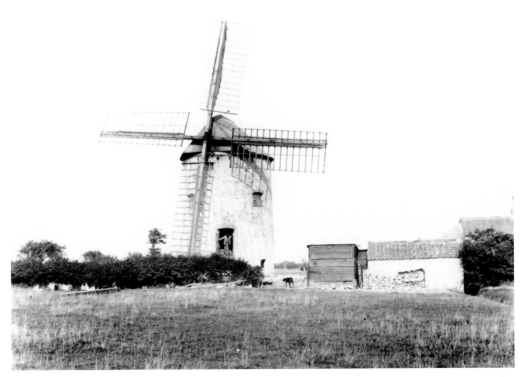

WORLE WINDMILL

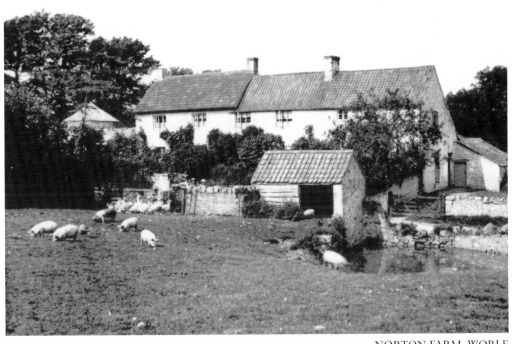

NORTON FARM, WORLE

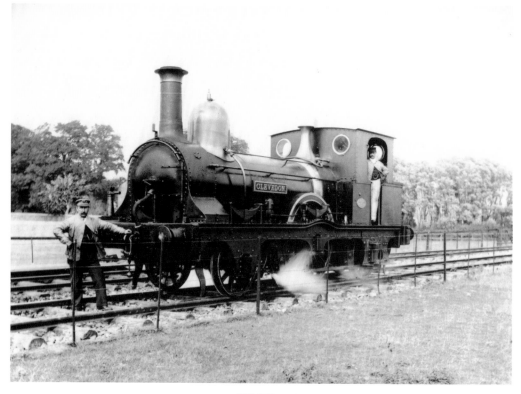

WESTON, CLEVEDON AND PORTISHEAD RAILWAY

A RAILWAY ACCIDENT

I do not know anywhere where the contrast between the old order and the new is more picturesquely shown than at Bathampton. The main line of the Great Western Railway and the Weymouth branch here meet at the little wayside station close to one of the most pleasing and thoroughly rural-looking churches that will be found anywhere out of a picture. No one can pass along the line without noticing its pretty ivy-mantled tower, and though the rest of the church is very modern it is in accordance with the old design, while in the graveyard around it repose many generations of quiet villagers who were wont to worship in this time-hallowed spot. The peaceful old-world associations which the church thus possesses side by side with the unrest, the haste and the danger of railway traffic, seem to illustrate the distinction that exists between the work of God and the work of man, and the preacher might point out therefrom how the element of peace is lacking in all worldly things.

It happened indeed on the particular occasion to which I am especially referring that the hateful whisper came by as we entered the church 'there's an accident on the line.' So at the conclusion of their peaceful devotions minster and congregation walked down the lane to the junction to see where large gangs of men were removing the gigantic debris of a heavily-laden luggage train scattered and shattered and piled up in every direction by its misspent energy as if Titans had been at play. It is only in such a spectacle as this that we see the amount of power which is employed in our service and which a slight flaw will turn to our destruction. The possible horrors of these occurrences are so well understood that the intelligence of one is never received without a painful shudder. Though no lives were lost on this occasion we learnt that this shock to an old and respected official in charge of the station at Bath had been fatal—on the receipt of the news his heart ceased to beat.

Church Rambler

MONTACUTE HILL

Few landmarks in south Somerset are more conspicuous than is that of St Michael's Mount under which lies the old-world village of Montacute. The hill rises immediately behind the parish church and the Abbey and overlooks Middlestreet, Bishopston, and the Borough, and indeed each cottage garden, however secluded, of the lovely hamlet. 'After the Hill of Senlac and the vanished choir of Waltham we may fairly place the wooded hill of Montacute,' wrote the historian Freeman. Small wonder therefore that Thomas Shoel, the poet, was so passionately fond of the hill and is rumoured to have sat for hours upon its crest contemplating the life of his natal village.

> *The leather dresser at his perch too stands,*
> *And the keen knife employs his busy hands.*
> *While the neat glover seated at the door*
> *Or in the porch, employs the busy hour.*

Or meditating upon the wider West Country prospects that open so spaciously to the view of the wayfarer from the summit of this green hill of legend and romance.

As children, when the floods were out in the Christmas holidays and the half of the county of Somerset would lie before us white as a sheet, there would often be good skating in the meadows of Ilchester, and I remember well when we were returning from one of these expeditions along the main street of the old Parliamentary Borough town noticing how Montacute Hill appeared precisely placed in the centre of the wintry horizon as though, in fact, it had been deliberately set to embellish the landscape outline so sharply segmented by the parallel roofs that bordered the old thoroughfare—the Roman road straight as a pike-staff, and in the exact centre of our vision five miles away the familiar pyramidal hill of our home. The form of a hill of so singular a symmetry must have been well known to the legionaries, and later to the Saxons, especially in those dark days when the fortifications of the Conqueror's 'insatiable brother' began to show themselves upon the hill's crest. Roger Bacon must have known its shape well, as also many a gaoler from the notorious 'Den' in their off hours; to say nothing of generations of humbler folk—waggoners trudging behind wains of loaded hay, drovers at the tails of shambling water-meadow bullocks fat as butter, white bonneted women with balanced buckets of well-water at their arm's ends, and children with marbles and coloured whip-tops in their pockets.

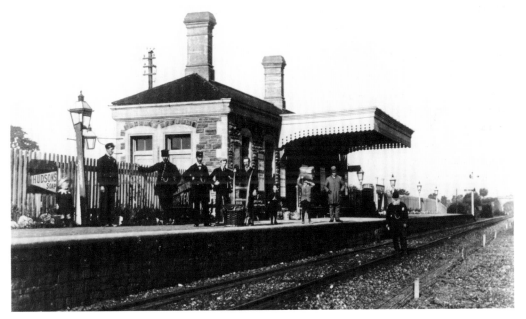

MONTACUTE STATION

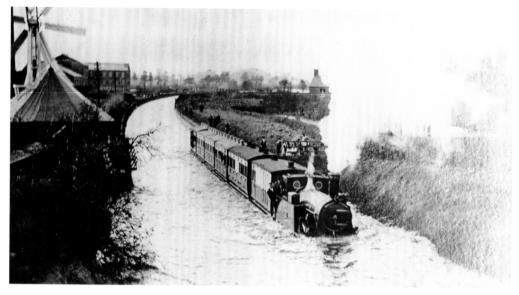

FLOODS, CREECH ST MICHAEL

If St Michael's hill has been a diurnal object of vision to the townsmen of Ilchester, how much more to the actual dwellers in Montacute! All the dead who for century after century have been gathered into the churchyard of St Catherine's, from the oldest grave to the newest grave, must have known and deeply loved its quiet presence so strong and so unchanging. What the eternal hills of the Promised Land were to the imagination of the dying and exiled Israel, and what the Acropolis was to the Athenians, Miles Hill, this symbol of the enduring earth, has been to the people of Montacute. How many Phelipses, lying now in their family vault near the church porch, must have looked up at its lofty height from the oriels of their proud gallery; how many quarrymen and gloving women must have glanced up at it through twilight window panes. Mrs William Phelips used to tell how a former lady of Montacute House, Dame Betty I think she was called, had herself planted the hill with the forest trees that flourished in so much glory at the end of the nineteenth century. Every afternoon she had carried acorns, chestnuts, or nursery slips to the cherished slopes. What a splendour, if the story is true, the lady's patient task bequeathed to later generations. Well do I remember the hill in its leafy magnificence. The winding trackway that led eventually to the tower was over-shadowed with timber of enormous proportions 'enfolding sunny spots of greenery'. The hill's top was crowned with Scotch firs—lofty, haggard trees that had confronted many an autumn gale and the tallest of which, a veritable forest king, was eventually struck down, a wild cross of Leodgaresburgh laid at its length, a mass of splintered deal for fools to wonder at.

How impressive an eminence it was in those days, the green mountain which in winter and in summer so utterly dominated the village of golden stones below. The great trees offered sanctuary to every kind of bird, but especially to rooks. Montacute Hill was famed for possessing the largest King-rookery in all Somerset and perhaps in all the west of England. In the winter thousands upon thousands of these birds would come here to roost. On wild autumn nights, at an hour when lamps were being lit, it was scarcely possible to hear oneself speak in the Montacute streets so great would be the clamour set up by the hosts of birds that were passing across the sky.

How we used to watch them from our nursery window—rising and falling, crying and calling, with outstretched ragged wings. It was impossible not to believe that each single one of these fowls was experiencing through bone and feather some strange ecstasy, each quill of them tingling to the whistling squalls, each air-filled bone of them full of the storm's frenzy, full of the frenzy of the great west wind, of the rainy wind, sweeping in from the sea, in from the Bishop rocks, and in from the uncharted wastes of the Atlantic, where masterless oceanic roarers thundered and screamed beneath a scudding sky of grey desolation. Before such tumults the huge trees would sway backwards and forwards delivering themselves of hoarse lamentations, their vexed branches thick clustered all night long with venerable hopper-crows whose beaks were polished

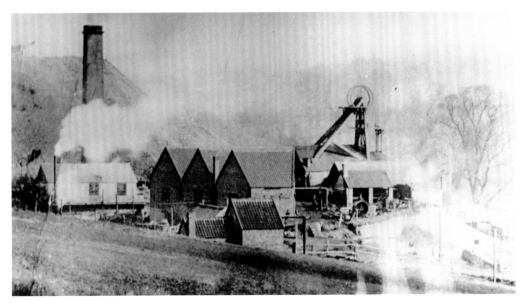

CAMERTON COLLIERY

white as silver by the constant exercise of corn-stealing from every ground between Avalon and Camelot and Babylon Hill and Pilsden Pen.

On calm evenings, when the smoke was rising straight and blue from the Montacute chimneys, the rocks would fly directly to their roosting place with scarce a caw, but should snow be falling they would be affected as much as they were by rainy winds. In such weather their voices would sound out of the sky with a terrifying resonance as the flakes fell thickly and more thickly—the multitudinous voices of these sapient birds, blacker in colour than Satan, who were performing some strange saraband of their own amidst the white falling goose-feathers from the Polden Hills.

Polden Hills are plucking their geese
Faster, faster, faster.

The magnificent timber had reached to its maturity and the Squire decided eventually to let loose the lumber men into that virginal abode of leaf and branch and bough. In a year's time the hill had been rendered as bald as a skull. Under this abomination of desolation the winter palace of the rook tribe was utterly destroyed. The birds were dispersed and began to form inconsequent colonies wherever they could find a few high trees—in the spinney by the Mill, in the beech trees surrounding John Scott's old house, and more especially in the half grown spruces that adorned the neighbouring height of Hedgecock. I am told that the tower of St Michael's Mount is once again hidden by timber, but for more than a quarter of a century it remained confronting sun, moon, and stars as lonely as a unicorn's horn.

Llewelyn Powys

RADSTOCK

'Frances Countess Waldegrave' is a name very familiar to railway travellers who often see it—upon coal trucks, for this lady almost set the fashion by which the peerage now owns without shame when it is connected with trade. Being the owner of coal-pits she trades in her own name, and is no less known in trade than she is conspicuous in the aristocratic circles of the metropolis. There are a number of coalpits at Radstock, and the town has all the ugly unwieldiness arising from rapid growth. The frowning chimneys which belch forth smoky clouds blackening and poisoning the fresh pure air of heaven, and the black heaps

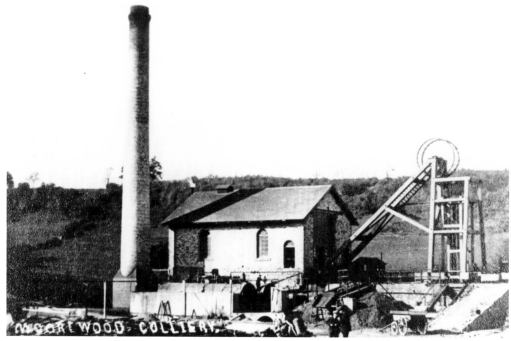

MOOREWOOD COLLIERY, OAKHILL

which load it with grimy dust, mark the mouths of the pits. Several prosperous tradesmen have rebuilt their houses in a substantial style, otherwise we have the buildings of a village in the midst of a town, clustering together at varying levels with the vaguest notion of streets. Again two railways run through the place but they have been laid level with the road and so two white gates keep back the horses while the engine is passing, and when that is gone your carriage may jump and jolt over the rails as best it can. However hateful these things may be to the mere theorist, I am of course aware that they are the natural outcome of the state of freedom in which we live, and I answer before they speak those readers in Radstock who will be offended at what I say, by adding that the closer inspection of the growth of new towns by the central government would without doubt be attended by other and greater evils than those which I have here grumbled at. But at the same time it is evident that hereafter large sums will be expended by the local authority on improvements to remedy the mistakes committed in the formation of the place.

Church Rambler

DULVERTON

The road turned and turned, but which ever way the Barle was always under us, and the red rock rose high at the side. This rock fractures aslant if worked, vast flakes come out, and the cleavage is so natural that until closely approached a quarry appears a cliff. Some got out in squares, or cut down straight leaves an artificial wall; these rocks cannot be made to look artificial, and if painted, a quarry would be certainly quite indistinguishable from a natural precipice. Entering a little town (Dulverton) the road is jammed tight between cottages; so narrow is the lane that foot passengers huddle up in doorways to avoid the touch of the wheels, and the windows of the houses are protected by iron bars like cages lest the splashboards should crack the glass. Nowhere in closest-built London is there such a lane—one would imagine land to be dear indeed. The farm labourers, filing homewards after their day's work, each carry poles of oak or faggots on their shoulders for their hearths, generally oak branches; it is their perquisite. The oak somehow takes root among the interstices of the stones of this rocky land. Past the houses the rush! rush! of the brown Barle rises again in the still evening air.

Richard Jefferies

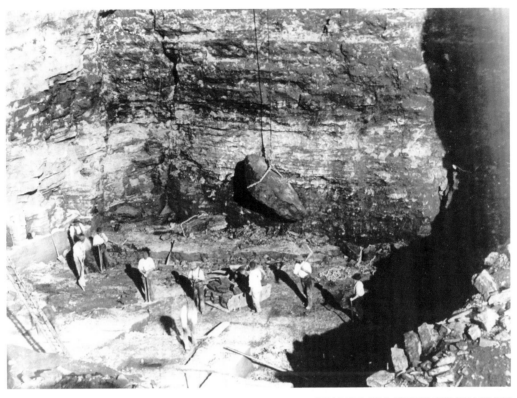

QUARRYMEN, STOKE SUB HAMDON

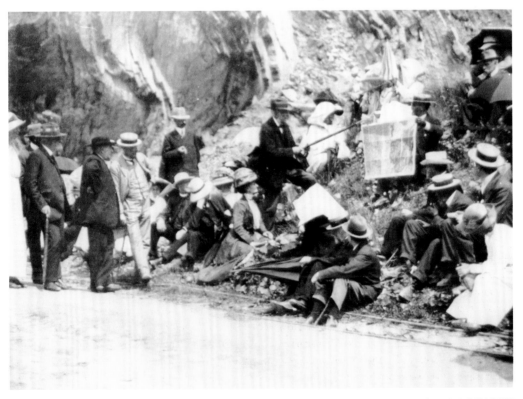

GEOLOGISTS AT WESTLEIGH QUARRY

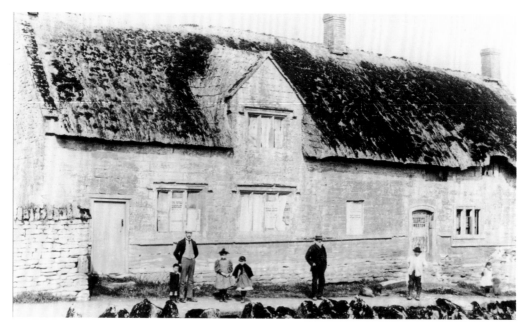

STOKE SUB HAMDON

THE LORD OF WRINGTON

A drive of about six miles further brought me to the lovely vale of Wrington. The great landowner in the parishes of Wrington and Burrington is the Duke of Cleveland, who, as a Whig politician, has in both Houses of Parliament given proof of considerable administrative ability. The wages of the labourers in this district were, on the average, 11s. or 12s. a week. There are, however, only a limited number of allotments, the Duke, or rather his agent, always inclining to increase the size of the large farms on his estate by throwing into them every available plot of ground. The great want in this district, a want which is very severely felt by the poor labourers, is for more cottages. The cottages on the estate generally are bad; the drainage, I was told, is also bad. Overcrowding is the natural consequence of the absence of proper accommodation for the labouring population. But the Duke or his agent will not build, although I was informed that there were 1,000 acres of land belonging to his grace, used as a common, but admirably adapted for sites for cottages. I was assured that the labourers had great difficulty in getting milk from the farms, the greater portion of the butter-milk being given to the farmers' pigs. This is a very important matter, because medical men consider milk to be such an excellent article of diet; and there is no doubt that milk, used with the bread of the labourer, constitutes an important item in his food; and considering his wretched fare, he ought to have an abundance of it. In fact, too often, I am sorry to observe, the rearing of horses, sheep, and cows, the housing of dogs, and the fattening of pigs, appear to be of far more importance to the farmer than the care of his labourers. The Duke of Cleveland has the reputation of being a liberal landlord. In that case, his residence in Wrington, which he has not visited more than twice, I believe, in six years, would be a blessing to the rural population. Even his grace's agent does not live in the place, but resides at Bath. What is, therefore, sadly wanted in the district is some representative of the noble Duke to look after the physical and social needs of the inhabitants. I was glad to find that there were in the place two excellent resident magistrates—Mr Long and Mr Edwards—who have exerted themselves admirably for the good of the inhabitants; but I was sorry to notice that the administration of justice was carried on in a small room in the village, instead of being conducted in a building specially adapted for the purpose. If the attention of the Duke of Cleveland were called to this circumstance he would no doubt remedy the matter. I must not forget to mention that Hannah More, who lived at the adjacent Barleywood lies, with her four sisters, buried in Wrington churchyard; nor that Wrington possesses perhaps the finest church tower in all Somersetshire, and, moreover, that it is the birthplace of John Locke.

F. G. Heath

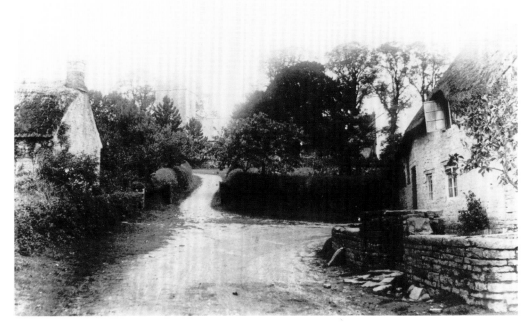

COMPTON DUNDON

WINSCOMBE

Coleridge considered the characteristic charm of Somersetshire to be 'its rurality.' Our village, we have said, was described by an American visitor as the prettiest he had seen in England. Comparisons are odious, and tastes differ; but if still prettier villages can be found in England, it would be hard to find one more thoroughly rural. Though it boasts of a 'street,' and even a 'square,' there is not a row of houses in the village. The street is without a shop, a foot-path, or a lamppost, and the square is simply the meeting of four lanes, with a small farm-house at each corner. The nearest approach to a shop is a little cottage with a few pipes and lollipops in the window, and an intimation over the door that the occupier is licensed to sell tobacco. There is not even a public-house or beer-shop in the village! An attempt was once made to supply this extraordinary deficiency, and a vermilion sign swung for some years from a small farm-house in the street, heralding the 'Rising Sun;' but the vermilion faded, the sign broke down, and so did the publican: the Rising Sun set, to rise no more.

The old village smithy, with mossy thatch, under a spreading pollard oak, has also gone. We miss the picturesque scene in winter evenings, when the red light of the forge, seen between intervening trees, shone upon the rustic figures, and the horses standing to be shod. We miss, too, the music of the harmonious blacksmith, for George, or Jarge, as he was called, could play the flute as well as wield the sledge hammer. He 'played the waits' at Christmas time, and sacrificed, occasionally, to Bacchus, as well as to Vulcan and Apollo. The old brown thatch, which for many years had proved, with the certainty of man's inheritance of trouble, that sparks fly upwards, and do not often come down alive, at last gave place to flaming tiles; the old ivy-grown oak was beheaded and felled, and the harmonious blacksmith went with his family to America, where, we hear, they are doing well.

Another thatched roof, on whose deep green mossy carpet the Virginia creeper used to spread its autumnal splendour is also gone. Time cures the rawness of even red tiles, and our village is not often disfigured by restorations. We lose more by neglect. The last twenty years have seen the end of many picturesque country objects: tumble-down cottages and sheds, fit only for sketching; old barns with dovecotes, ferny mossy walls, and rustic gates, the very originals of the old lithographic copies of our childhood, before 'free-hand' copies were invented by pattern designers to turn the amusement of drawing into vexation of spirit. A wall of the old tithe barn is still standing, but sadly marred by repair; the village pound has been lately improved away: near its

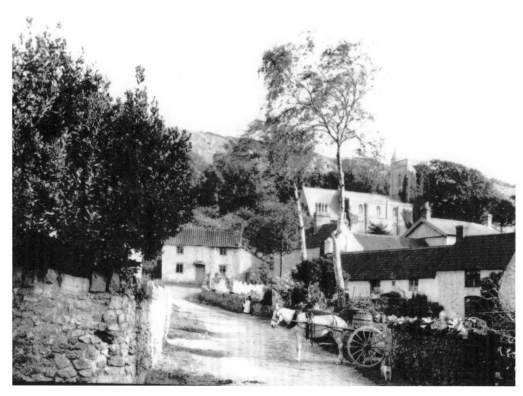

KEWSTOKE

site is a new cow-house, in a situation meet for nobler residents than even Court cows. The Court itself, the former abode of the Fraternity of the Blessed Virgin, has been lately 'restored,' and so thoroughly that, but for unbroken habitation, it might be called rebuilt. The fine old elms that used to shade it, and spread their boughs across the road, were felled some years ago, for fear of their falling on the old house. On the ascent of the hill, and opposite the Court, is the vicarage; its pretty garden and sloping lawns adjoining the churchyard: which brings us to the end of the village, and its crowning glory, the village church.

From the brook, looking up the street, with the church and its yew tree at the end, backed by the steep green hill, the village is a picture worthy an artist's skill. A more general, and even more picturesque view, including Crooks Peak, may be taken from the railway bridge, and a more distant one from Sidcot.

Theodore Compton

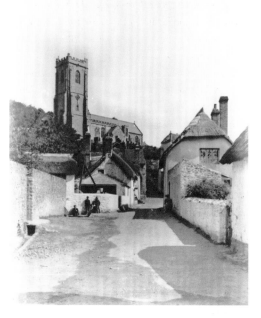

MINEHEAD

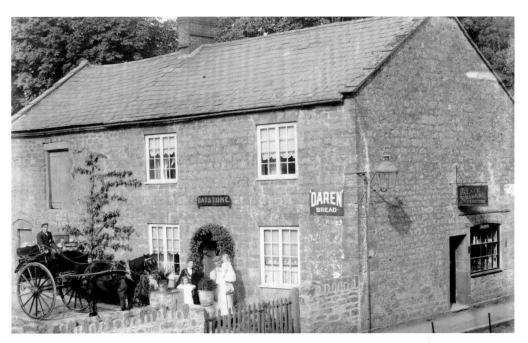

SOUTH PETHERTON

THE VILLAGE SHOP

Though our village is without assembly-room of any kind, except the parish church, and the whole parish is without either lawyer, doctor or dissenting minister, the central hamlet of Woodborough has a Railway Hotel and a Congregational Chapel, as well as the Board School, the Post Office, a Literary and Scientific Institute and Temperance Hall, besides a steam saw-yard and two smithies. The principal shop and two others are also here, and more than one deserving widow has opened what some call a coffee tavern, others a toffee cavern.

HM's Post Office is carried on at the principal shop. 'Man wants but little here below:' let us see how much of that little can be got at our shop. The first objects that catch the eye, here, as at similar shops the wide world over, are those variously decorated cubical cases, which prove not only the universal taste for biscuits, but the fertility of invention in their manufacture and nomenclature. Next to the twice-baked form of the staff of life, in conspicuous importance, are the announcements of HM's. Post-Master General, on a screen partly concealing the mysteries of that department; which, when spelt by th' unlettered muse, teach the rustic customer on what days, and by what outlandish routes, his communications will be despatched to Nijni Novogorod, Yokohama, and other familiar places. Here, of course, may be purchased, at all prices, from a halfpenny upwards, those variously tinted portraits of the Sovereign, which transport all they stick to from Woodborough to New Zealand, or any other part of the world. Between the reading and writing departments is the counter for stationery and drapery, where you may buy pens, ink and paper, valentines and Christmas cards when in season, smock frocks, shirts and socks, and the numberless 'things' requisite and necessary to adorn that form divine which when unadorned is, after all, adorned the most. On a shelf opposite the door is a display of crockery, chiefly for facilitating that which some unknown author, often supposed to be apostolic, declared to be 'next to godliness.' As the body is next to the soul, bodily cleanliness may be fairly put next to spiritual purity. The shelf below is more attractive to the young. Sweetmeats allure the tender mind, and, if nursery morals be sound, spoil the teeth; but here are other bottles to counteract the ill-effects of lollies and bullseyes; the bane and antidote are both before us, as in the days of Cato, and the Cato street conspiracy. The other end of the shop is devoted to grocery and the provision trade. Here you may supply your nearly free breakfast table with tea, coffee, cocoa, sugar, milk and cream, bread and butter, eggs and bacon, sardines and sausages, herrings, potted meats, marmalade; and your lunch or early dinner with peas for soup, pork and veal, cheese, flour, rice, currants and raisins, apples, oranges and lemons, prunes and

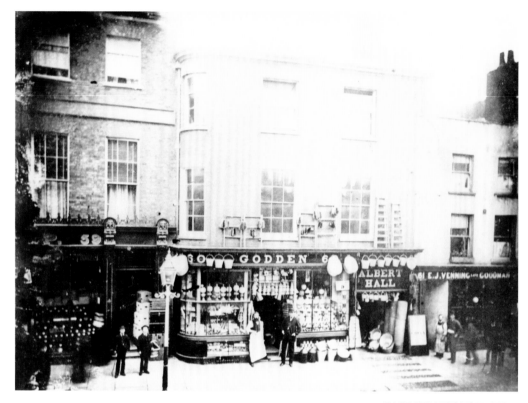

EAST STREET, TAUNTON

figs, and Brown and Polson. Over your head hang boots and shoes with formidable hobnails and iron heels, intermingled with spades and shovels, brushes and brooms, baskets and buckets, candles and curry-combs; in short, an inventory of all the articles in the shop would contain something for every letter in the alphabet: let us try. Arrowroot, Boots and butter, Corduroy and comforters, Dips and dust-shovels, Eatables without end, Frills and frying-pans, Geese and gridirons, Hams and halters, Ink and irons, Knives and ketchup, Lodgings and lollypops, Medicines and Nutmegs, Oatmeal and Pitchforks, Quills and Ribbons, Soap and Treacle, Umbrellas and Vinegar, Wax, eXtracts, Youths' clothing, and Zoedone, with other articles too numerous to mention.

Our shopkeeper is active and industrious, but not grasping or greedy. As a farmer he can take the rough with the smooth without looking sour. If the weather do not suit one crop, he thinks it is just right for another. As postmaster, if his letter-carrier falls sick or lame, he mounts his horse and delivers the letters himself. If he is sometimes disposed to complain that his neighbours' poultry tread down his mowing-grass, or injure his fallen apples, he remembers that they do good to his field and orchard ten months out of twelve, and that, putting one thing against another, he might have a worse neighbour. . .

Theodore Compton

THE DRAGON EMPORIUM

In these villages, two hundred miles from London, and often far from the rail, some of the conditions resemble those in the United States where, instead of shops, 'stores' supply every article from one counter. So here you buy everything in one shop; it is really a 'store' in the American sense. A house which seems amid fields is called 'The Dragon;' you would suppose it an inn, but it is a shop, and has been so ever since the olden times when every trader put out a sign. The sign has gone, but the name remains.

Richard Jefferies

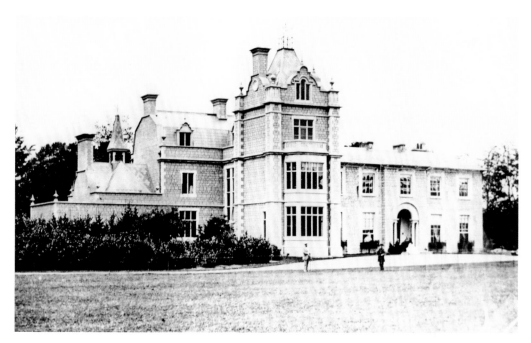

COSSINGTON GRANGE

HOUSE PARTY

To H. T. Baker   Mells Park,
                                    Frome,
                                    15 July 1900

On Saturday I came here by the route which you sketched for me—Everything went well and I arrived exactly at the right time owing to the place being five miles from the station—It is a typically comfortable English country house in an Elizabethan Park full of magnificent trees. The house itself is crowded with priceless pictures, which I don't appreciate—my hostess, a clever and charming woman, having been one of Burne-Jones' earliest models. There is no-one here of consuming interest except Haldane who has been in magnificent form—especially when he described to us how the High Church party had come to him to ask him to argue before the Archbishop the case for incense, asperges and the reservation of the sacrament: it is one of the most magnificent situations ever imagined and he described it in language worthy of Gibbon. There is also a very nice little Tory MP called Stirling Maxwell, and Bron's filthy cousin Wallop,—a lank and indifferent creature with a ginger moustache, who, I confess is something of an enigma to me. He is supposed to take no interest in anything but the intrigues of fashionable women, but he talked to me with apparent knowledge and enthusiasm about Lord Burghclere's translation of the Georgics, and apart from

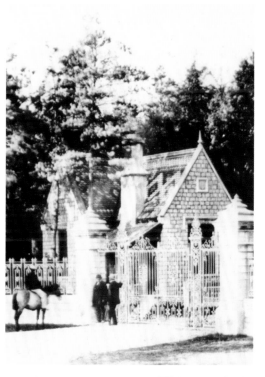

THE NEW LODGE

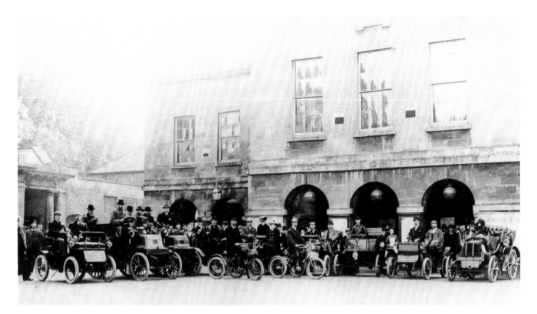

WELLS

that never once opened his mouth to anyone except to say that his cousin married Shaw-Lefevre, when Haldane made a disparaging remark about Shaw-Lefevre's sister. The only other person of any interest is one Mrs Gaskell, who is pleasant and passably clever, with whom I had a good talk about Meredith. But beyond doubt the really best thing about my visit—the thing that almost compensated for a five mile walk round the Park which my host took me this evening to explain the various qualities and characteristics of his unique collection of pines, in which he is a specialist—was the bathing. In front of the house is a terrace, beneath which after a steep fall of 100 feet runs a stream which has been dammed into a considerable lake about 1/4 mile in length by 200 yds in breadth, covered with waterlilies and fringed with bulrushes, where they bathe: it is very beautiful; but not so beautiful as the two daughters of the house aged 17 and 18 [in fact 15 and 17]—the elder of whom—tho she does not happen to appeal very strongly to me—is about as perfect a specimen of female beauty as I have ever seen.—About ½ past 4—just before tea Haldane suggested a bathe: no-one but himself and this lovely girl seemed keen about it: however we all went down to the lake as spectators and were amply rewarded. Haldane is an imperfect but courageous performer in the water and to see his immense but stately figure clad in a very scanty bathing dress and recklessly precipitating from dizzy altitudes into this green and flowery pond was really exquisite: the quiet slowness and dignity with which he put himself in the most ridiculous situations proved to me more conclusively than anything else could have done the real bigness of the man—to see this vast white mass with the brain of Socrates and the shape of Nero executing his absurd antics from a thin plank which bent double under his weight and sporting fantastically in the water with a divinely beautiful girl no whit abashed recalled the sunniest days of the Roman decline. Finally he came out and after lurking coyly in the bushes for a few minutes reappeared clad in nothing but a bath-towel and a panama hat and joined us at tea on the lawn where he was soon explaining the theory and history of Buddhism—its superiority to Christianity and its weakness as a practical religion—to a host of local spinsters who had flocked in for food and gossip. It was magnificent. At 11.30 p.m. he left in a carriage for Bath 15 miles off having to be in the courts at 10 tomorrow and in the train all tomorrow night and the night after—on his way up and down to Edinburgh where he is pleading on Tuesday. He is a marvellous man, and never loses flesh through it all. I go up to town tomorrow and to Wanborough on Tuesday. Hey nonny nonny! I like this life.

Raymond

PS. This letter looks longer than it is.

Raymond Asquith

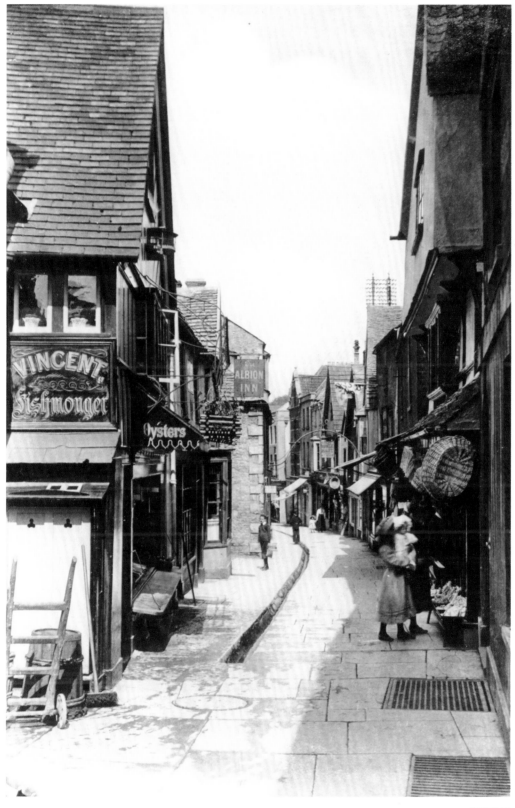

FROME

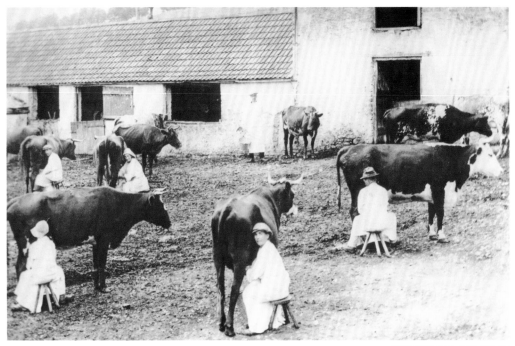

BATCOMBE, MILKING

FARM VISIT

The first item on Thursday morning's programme—a visit to Milton Clevedon—was one which had been eagerly anticipated, Mr Cannon having achieved remarkable fame as a maker of the highest class of Cheddar cheese. The fact that he has won £2,300 in prizes in the last 15 years indicates the skill with which his dairy operations have been so long conducted. The farm at Milton Clevedon, lying high and dry on the north-western slope of a hill, has been in his occupation since 1887. The capital herd of cows, numbering 50 or thereabouts, are mostly Shorthorn crosses. Mr Cannon's practice is to select a good cross-bred dam, which has been proved to be a good milker, and mate her with a pure-bred Shorthorn bull. Altogether the cattle were considered to be a creditable lot, possessing good milking qualities. It is not the custom to measure each cow's milk, but the pail is carefully watched, in order to note any sudden falling off. The dairy, in which on our arrival Mrs Cannon and a daughter (the latter a sister of the teacher at the Butleigh Cheese School) were at work with the curd, is a remarkably well-arranged apartment, which, as well as the appliances it contained, greatly reflected upon Mr Cannon's judgment and experience. The floor, composed of large stone slabs, is so laid as to give a fall to a gutter running along the centre. To avoid the necessity of women lifting large weights, there is an arrangement whereby the requisite pressure on the curd is obtained by placing lead blocks into position by means of a small pulley. Throughout the dairy work nothing is done at haphazard, but all measuring and testing is done with the greatest possible accuracy. Questioned as to the secrets of his successful results, Mr Cannon replied, 'I have no secrets beyond cleanliness and accuracy.' Hence pains are always taken to see that all the utensils used are free from crevices, that the thermometers are absolutely reliable, and, in short, to do everything possible to ensure uniformity. In every department perfect order and cleanliness were marked. The scalding is done by means of a steam pipe from a large boiler placed outside the dairy; and the whey is taken away in a pipe to a tank at a considerable distance. The upstairs cheese-room is fitted with shelves, heated by a stove in the centre, and the ceiling is boarded in substitution for the original plaster. As already indicated, the curd was being stirred in the whey when the party arrived. This was from 140 gallons of night's and morning's milk produced by the 48 cows actually in milk. The plan adopted is to rennet at 84°, to first scald at 88°, and the second time at 92° to 94°. After renneting, the milk remains for three-quarters of an hour, when the curd is cut into pieces about two inches square. In this state it remains for about 15 minutes,

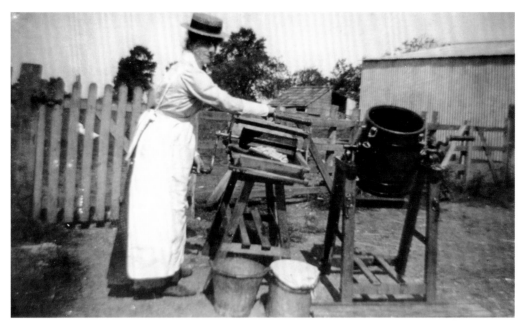

BUTTERMAKING

when the breaker is used to reduce it to pieces as small as a pea. It is allowed to settle, and a portion of the whey is then heated so as to bring the bulk up to 88°, stirring for a quarter of an hour. More whey is taken off for the second scald to 92°, or a little higher. The curd is allowed to settle for a quarter of an hour, when the whey is drawn off and put into leads, the cream being skimmed off the next morning and churned once a week—producing an average of 6 lbs butter. The curd is piled in the centre of the vat and cut into squares, turned, and covered with cloths. After a while it is put into the cooler, broken in lumps, again cut twice, and turned until ripe enough to vat. It may be interesting to state that the cheese made on the day of the Association's visit was duly branded with a view to future identification, and purchased for sale in sample form at the coming Dairy Show.

Journal of the British Dairy Farmers Association

THE CHEESE SCHOOL AT BUTLEIGH

The cheese school at Butleigh conducted by the Bath and West of England Society. . . is on the farm of Mr H. G. Bethell (Lower Rock Farm), 30 of whose cows supply milk for the school. In addition, the milk of 22 cows belonging to Mr James Hunt, on the adjoining Bridge Farm, is dealt with. Mr Gibbons, the active dairy steward of the Bath and West of England Society, explained that this school is the fourth that has been held in the county for the teaching of cheesemaking, and altogether it has been attended by over 200 pupils.

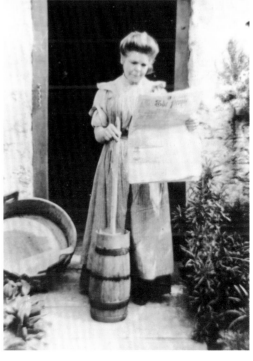

BUTTERMAKING, NORTH WOOTTON

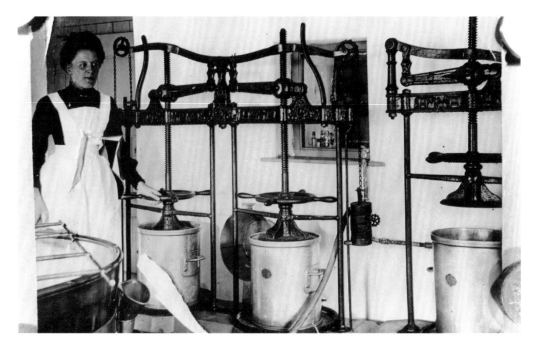

CHEESE PRESSES

As he was careful to point out, the arrangements were of a simple and ordinary character, such as seen in connection with the average cheese-making homestead, there being an absence of all expensive buildings or appliances. For instance, the milk heater and the outside boiler cost only about 20 guineas. In fact, the system taught is such as might be followed in any home dairy; the object of the school being, of course, to raise the general quality of the cheese made in the district. Mr Lloyd, who conducts experiments at the school, has a room close to the dairy, and attends about once a week; while an assistant, Mr Hewitt, is always on the spot. With their aid investigations are constantly in progress with a view to solve some of the problems that at present trouble and perplex cheesemakers. Up till now the work of the school has been eminently successful, the quality of the cheese turned out having been very praiseworthy. It is satisfactory to learn that the pupils now remain very much longer than they originally did. At first they came for a week or a fortnight, but now many of them stay for a complete month. Mr Gibbons expressed his belief that Miss Cannon, the teacher, would just as readily have pupils who knew nothing whatever about cheese-making, as those who had long practised it; and on this point the lady in question remarked that those who were entirely ignorant of cheese-making were, perhaps, the best pupils, because they had nothing to unlearn and were quite free from prejudices. At the school about 7 lbs of whey butter are made weekly, realising, as a rule, 2d. per lb less than butter made from cream skimmed from whole milk. On the day of our visit about 147 gallons of milk was being dealt with. The morning temperature of the dairy was 60°. Rennet was added at 84°, at 6.38 a.m., 2 gallons of sour whey being also used. The first scald is 88°, and the second 92°. Every cheese is weighed when it goes into the cheese-room, and the weight when it is sent to the factor is also recorded. All the cheese made since the school was commenced has been sold to one man, who has paid from 65s. to 70s. per cwt. of 112 lbs. Last year the average yield was 1 lb of cheese to 1 gallon of milk. The price paid for the milk was 6½d. a gallon, the farmer receiving back the whey, and it was found that the cheese sales just covered the cost of the raw material.

Journal of the British Dairy Farmers Association

EVERCREECH DAIRY FACTORY

Passing through Evercreech, a halt was made at the dairy factory started nearly two years ago by Mr Hargreaves, who has recently disposed of it to Mr George Jackson, of Birmingham and elsewhere. From

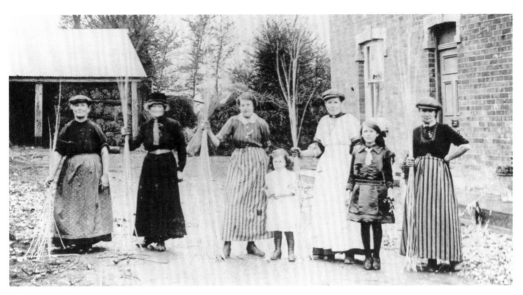

WILLOW STRIPPERS, LYNG

information kindly supplied by Mr Cross, the manager, it appears that about 400 gallons of milk are daily supplied by eight farmers, who are paid 5½d. per gallon in summer, and 7d. to 8d. in the winter months. About 85 per cent of the separated milk is taken back by the farmers at 1d. per gallon. Milk is delivered once a day, except in very hot weather. In May it took 26 lbs of milk to produce a pound of butter, the price of which was Is. 2d. per lb. It goes to Manchester, London, Birmingham, and other places. It is drysalted, at the rate of about 2 per cent of salt. A certain quantity of skim cheese is made, and the price realised, 2½d. per lb, fairly represents its value. The particulars which follow are taken from a local paper:

> The factory has been fitted throughout by the Dairy Supply Company with the view of dealing with 2,000 gallons of milk a day. A considerable number of farmers are availing themselves of the advantage it offers.

Journal of the British Dairy Farmers Association

GROWING WITHIES

The railway cut across the moor. The water-traffic slowly dwindled and now is almost dead. For awhile there were hard times around Athelney, but at last the very thing which wrought the mischief brought the cure. The train opened up distant markets for the withies which flourish upon the low country all around, and today everybody is more or less a withy-merchant and well to do.

Along the rhines, which intersect this low country and serve instead of hedges to part the fields, are rows of leaning pollard willows. There is a saying that a willow will buy a horse whilst any other tree is paying for the halter. Once in three or four years the heads of the pollards are cropped, but the main of the withies for basket making are grown in withybeds, of which there are hundreds of acres upon any one of the large moors.

The small withy-grower takes a plot upon a long lease; plants it with willow-rods—for any stick, if the ground be wet enough, will grow; and hoes it clean from weeds like a field of turnips. To most people a willow is a willow and there is an end to it, but there are a score or more of varieties, all known by name like orchard trees.

At first the crop is meagre, but year by year the shoots are more and more, and when the roots are strong and tough and the withies cut, they can turn cattle in to trample down and bite off the weeds and thus save hoeing. The long straight wands are bound in bundles called bolts, and a bolt of withies should measure three feet one inch round at the butt. These must stand upright in pits of water until the rind will slip and they are ready for stripping.

Then through all the spring every woman of Athelney, young and old, and all the children too, are busy as bees.

At first, the noonday sunlight glints through a dark trelliswork of unclad branches meeting overhead; then the blossom comes, a cloud of flowers that ripen and drop softly down upon the ground; and next, in leafy June there grows a mystery of cool green shade. But however you catch the withy-stripper at work there is the change and charm of a simply natural industry out of doors.

The withy-stripper has no tool but an upright post, in the top of which, close together, two flat irons, very like pieces of hoop-iron, are firmly fixed. The whole contrivance, by name a withy-break, stands about the height of a hurdle. Between the iron are two little steels which clip the withy and tear away the rind as it is dragged through. Some of the tapering sticks are ten feet long and straight as fishing-rods; but the steels, closing tightly from the spring of the irons, rend them clean from butt to tip, and the willows are so tough and free to bend that Athelney maidens deftly strip the longest without stepping back.

There is a new subject for a painter in this family group.

Under their orchard bower they stand, their figures clear against a whitewashed cottage wall. A mother staid, with slender maids grown up and slips of girls with hair half down their backs, and still a little one or two at play, no higher than the break. To their right hands, leaning against a rail, is spread an untied bolt of willows fresh and green, and on the ground upon the left of each a pile of wands just stripped and shining clean as ivory. In front there is a heap of dull green rind. They let it dry and stack it up for firing by-and-bye. And all the while as they sway to and fro they laugh and talk.

There is no other sound, but the sigh of the unceasing ripple below the river-wall, the whisper of the west wind to the leaves, the chattering sparrows on the roof and somewhere on a spray above their heads the chaffinch singing, 'Pink! pink! pink. Pretty little dear.'

When the withy is peeled it must be put in the sun to dry, and then it is ready for the basket-maker. The sticks are set out, leaning all along the wall or hedgerow by the road, and very nice they look. Some of them are coloured buff, and to do this they are boiled before being stripped. Nothing foreign is used, for the dye is in the rind.

But should you wish to become a successful withymerchant, kindly note: Vor buffs the water mus' be on the bwoil when you do clap 'em in. Jus' the very zame as you do do wi' cabbage—look-y-zee?

Walter Raymond

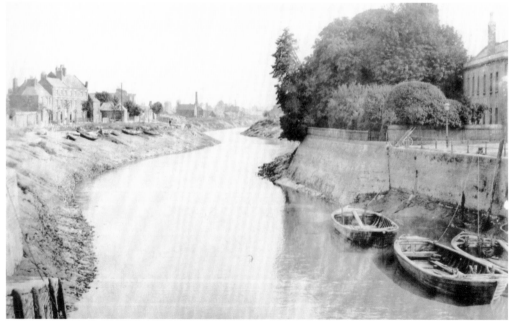

ATHELNEY

There is no village of Athelney, only by right the island and the farm, and these form part of the charming moorland parish of Lyng. But the railway station close by has been called by the ancient name; and to the casual visitor, the cottages along the tow-path of the Tone are Athelney and nothing else.

At a glance it is not tempting, this tidal river, in one part straight as a line, and again winding between deep banks of slimy mud left bare. It seems to be low-water all the time; only a spring tide can reach so far from the sea and cover for a while the dark brown mire. A great black barge, broken and abandoned, lies high and dry, aslant against the side. Another which still makes a journey, may-be once a month, rides at her mooring in the river-course. Here and there, down the steep side from the tow-path are steps of stone leading to long flat-bottomed boats of primitive design. Upon the river-wall are houses, many of which appear but huts until upon a closer study you find that they are homes. You cannot fall in love at first sight with the Tone as you may with the dashing Barle, or any clear maiden stream that sings and dances over yellow gravel stones. But as you look, the quaintness of it grows. You get a palate for the place, as it were, until at last it becomes delightful.

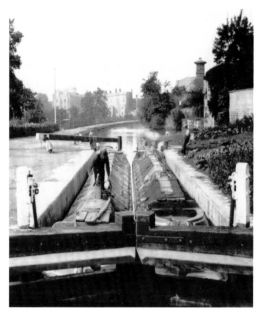

KENNET AND AVON CANAL, BATH

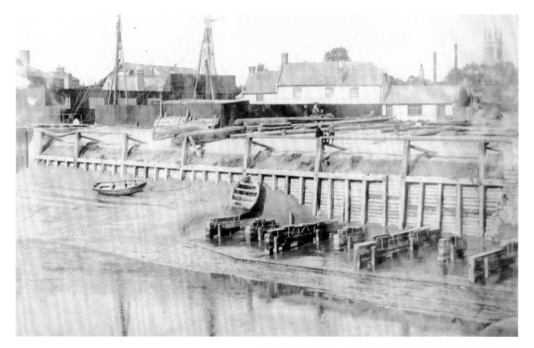

BRIDGWATER DRY DOCK AND RIVER PARRETT

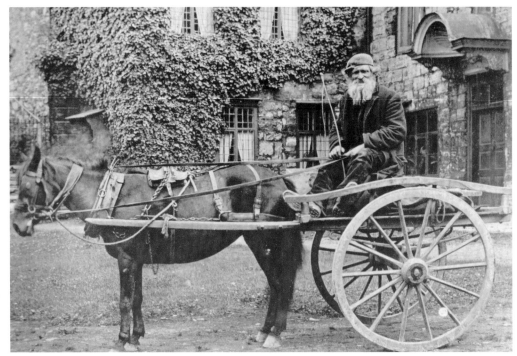

BROOMSQUIRE, TAUNTON

It was a Paradise of squatters in times gone by, and therein lies its greatest charm today.

Between the river and the road there is the tow-path and the wall—a 'ward-wall' as the good folk mention with some pride. A wall upon the moors is not a thing of stones and mortar, but a good stout mound—a dam, broad as a highway and strong enough to hold back a flood like an inland sea. A 'ward-wall' moreover stands upon a sure and immovable foundation of British law, being placed there under an award.

Along this strip, for a good two miles or more, are houses of all shapes and sizes, with outlets to the tow-path and riverbank, and gardens opening upon the road. Many of them also have bits of orchard too, may-be a dozen trees or more. For nearly every man in Athelney, as we may as well call the place, lives in his own house. His forefather most likely raised a mud hut upon the wall and railed a bit of garden round. He thatched his roof with sedge cut from the rhines, those deep ditches that intersect the moors, and there he lived without ostentation but with secret inward pride. Nobody bothered about him. Indeed, in those days he was welcomed there; for both the Tone and Parrett were busy thoroughfares for barges then, and he worked upon the river all his life. But bit by bit his mansion grew. He set a hedge against the road and planted an apple tree. And thus after some years he gained a solid holding and left it to his son.

There is an idea in many country minds that if a house can only be built and inhabited without interference on unenclosed land it will stand. As village wisdom gravely expresses it over a quart cup: 'If you could but put un up unbeknown, look-y-zee, in one night and live in un by marnen—zo sure as the light he's your'n.'

Walter Raymond

THE ISLAND OF THE PRINCES

About a mile from the meeting of the rivers Tone and Parrett is a rising ground, so gentle that, in latter spring, when grassy moors put on their wealth of glistening buttercups and shine like sheets of gold, the eye, looking from some distant knoll, can scarcely find it from the level plain.

A homestead, with dark stalls around a barton pitched with stones stands just at the foot of the slope. Hard by are hayricks and a stack or two of straw, and, sweetest of all sights in Somerset, an orchard out in

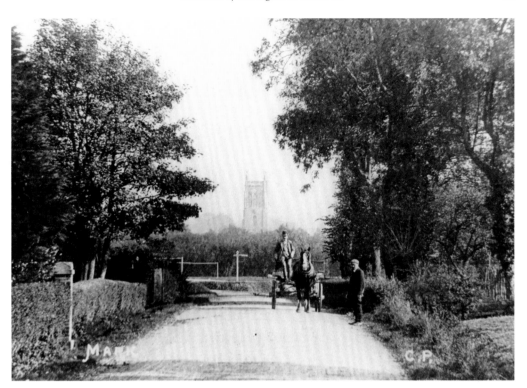

MARK

bloom. Here and there an early 'Pouncer,' its blossom lying like snow on the lush grass beneath, is turning to green leaf; but in the main the trees 'be vull o' blowth,' except the little 'Horner,' most renowned of cider apples, which comes last and waits in winter black, whilst all the rest, in joy to meet the spring, are robed in silver and in pink.

There is a row of elms with new-fledged leafage fresh and green, a group of willows and some poplars tall as spires.

Along the side a herd of dairy cows, bright dabs of colour red and white, stand steadfast gazing all one way, or lie at rest, glad with the fresh spring growth, and ruminate. Upon the top a flock of ewes is scattered in the sun. And there enclosed with iron rails is a small obelisk, bearing the following inscription:

King Alfred the Great, in the year of our Lord 879, having been defeated by the Danes, fled for refuge to the forest of Athelney, where he lay concealed from his enemies for the space of a whole year. He soon after regained possession of his throne and in grateful remembrance of the protection he had received under the favour of Heaven erected a monastery on this spot and endowed it with all the lands contained in the Isle of Athelney. To perpetuate the memorial of so remarkable an incident in the life of that illustrious prince this edifice was founded by John Slade, Esq., of Mansel, the proprietor of Athelney Farm and Lord of the Manor of North Petherton.

A.D. 1801.

This is all the pilgrim can find to help recall the memory of the great Saxon king, his hiding-place and wanderings, and the triumph that came to him at last. Nor today in spring or summer is it easy to picture this ancient Isle of Nobles. Only when the swollen river breaks its wall and winter floods arise all round—when the west Sedgemoor is a swamp, Stanmore a sea, and Southlake 'drowned' as they say, does the Island of Athelney, one-half the size of a small farm, stand out alone, as it stood in the old fen, and justify for a week or so its claim to the title.

Walter Raymond

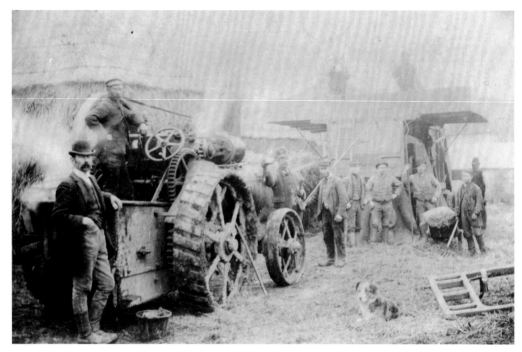

THRESHING TACKLE

VILLAGE LIFE

A hundred years since, before steam, the corn was threshed out by the flail—a slow, and consequently expensive process. Many efforts were made to thresh quicker. Among others, wooden machines were put up in some of the villages, something resembling a water-wheel placed horizontally. This was moved by horses walking round and round, and drove machinery in the barn by belt or shafting. The labourers, greatly incensed—for they regarded threshing by the flail as their right—tried to burn them, but the structures were guarded and still exist. Under the modern conditions of farming they are still found useful to cut chaff, crack corn, and so on. The ancient sickle is yet in use for reaping in Somerset; the reapers sharpen it by drawing the edge through an apple, when the acid bites and cleans the steel. While we were sauntering through a village one morning, out rushed the boys from school, and instantly their tongues began to wag of those things on which their hearts were set. 'I know a jay's nest,' said one; 'I know an owl's nest,' cried a second; a third hastened to claim knowledge of a pigeon's nest. It will be long before education drives the natural love of the woods out of the children's hearts. Of old time a village school used to be held in an ancient

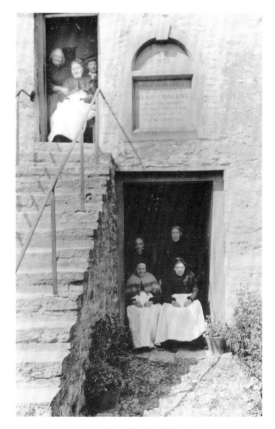

ALMSHOUSES, CANNINGTON

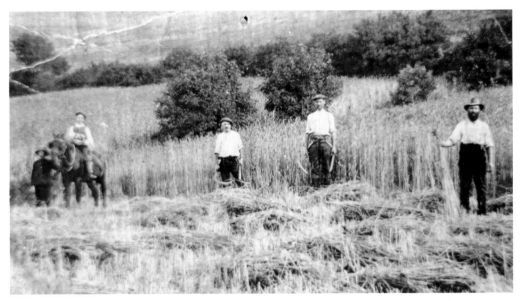

HARVESTING OATS, WICK

building, the lower part of which was occupied as almshouses. Underneath the ancient folk lived as best they might, while the young folk learned and gave their class responses, or romped on the floor overhead. The upper part of the building belonged to one owner; the lower part to another landlord. It came about that the roof decayed, and the upper owner suggested to the lower owner that they should agree in bearing the cost of repairs. Upon which the owner of the basement remarked that he contemplated *pulling his part down*.

Richard Jefferies

POVERTY AMONG PLENTY

Deeply embosomed in the heart of the Mendip Hills, about twelve miles to the east of Weston-super-Mare, and about the same distance to the south-west of Bristol, lies the Vale of Wrington. Proceeding from Weston-super-Mare, the road to this delightful vale runs to the north of the Mendips, through the most beautiful and romantic scenery. As far as the eye can reach, on every side, stretch rich pasture lands, the various and exquisite tints of the May green contrasting charmingly with the golden flowers of the buttercup. Even on the hill-sides the pastures extend, only broken here and there by thickets of trees, the dark and almost invisible green of which lends a sombre majesty to the scene. Numbers of sheep and oxen, all along the line of route, are seen grazing on the pastures. The county is celebrated for its dairy

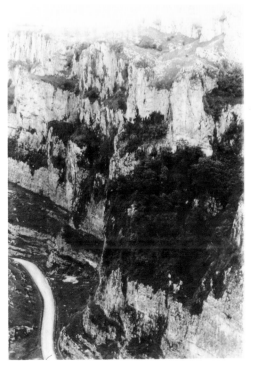

CHEDDAR GORGE

produce, the celebrated Cheddar cheese, which is furnished from the neighbouring Cheddar valley, being widely known for its excellence. Driving from Weston-super-Mare to the village of Wrington, soon after my arrival in Somersetshire, I endeavoured to make the best use of my opportunity of enquiring into the condition of the peasants. When about a mile or two away from the first-mentioned place I stopped and accosted an old labourer, and made some pertinent enquiries about himself. He told me he was seventy-seven years of age, and had worked as a farm labourer in that part of the country nearly all his life. He was then receiving 7s. a week, out of which he had to pay 1s. 6d. a week for his cottage. He had received somewhat better wages when younger; but I could not help thinking it hard that a hale old man (for my informant had all the appearance of being one) could not, after more than sixty years of hard toil, obtain more for food and clothes than the miserable pittance of 5s. 6d. a week.

F. G. Heath

BRENT KNOLL

If there is any place in the West any one should make a point of seeing, it is Brent Knoll. The air on the top of the Knoll is of the most invigorating kind, and the view on all sides is very striking; embracing first the great alluvial plain, with all its wonderful richness, reaching up to Glastonbury Tor; and on all sides, except that towards the Mendip—here in its finest outline, and including the Cheddar Cliffs—extending from forty to fifty miles. Another reason why Brent Knoll should be visited is because at its foot lies the home of that distinguished ornament of the Church of England, the Venerable Archdeacon DENISON. The likelihood is that sometime during the afternoon you will find him about the vicarage grounds, or in the church, which alone is worth seeing. But about that we shall have more to say a little later on. As for the Archdeacon he is a most genial gentleman, and if you are not particularly backward he will very readily enter into a pleasant chat with you.

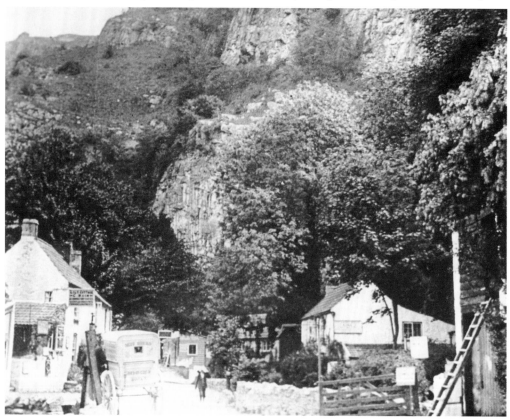

CHEDDAR

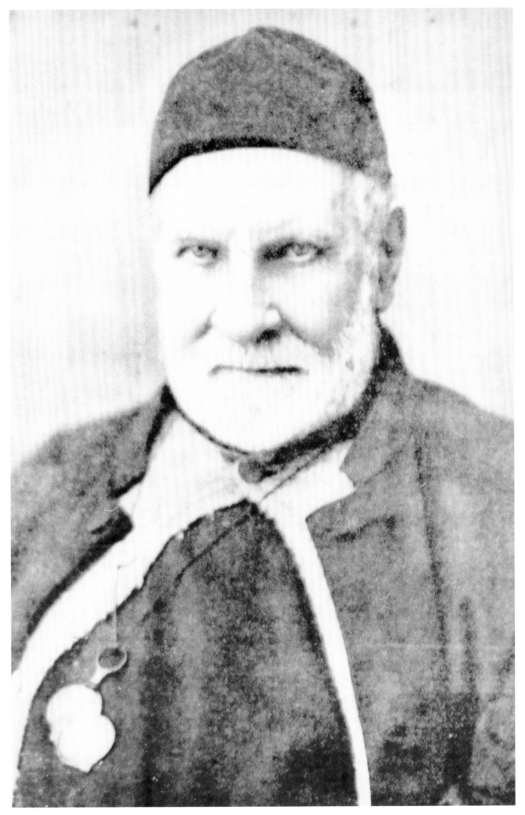

ARCHDEACON DENISON

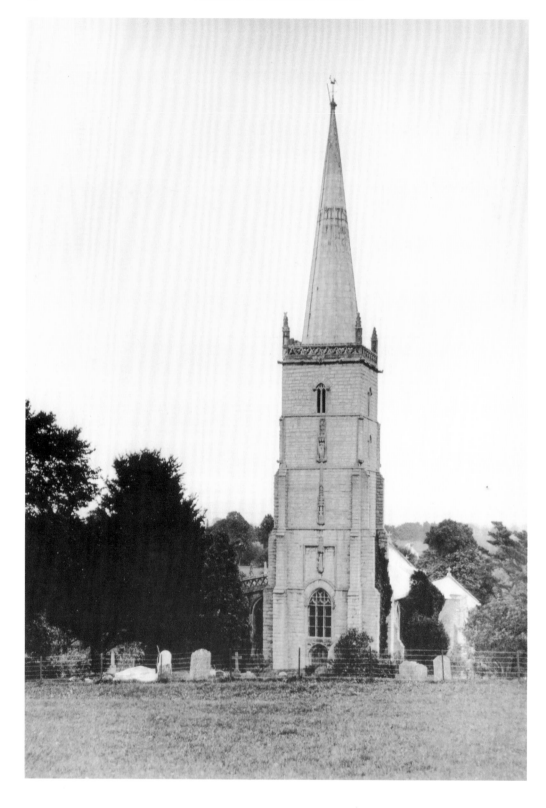

EAST BRENT

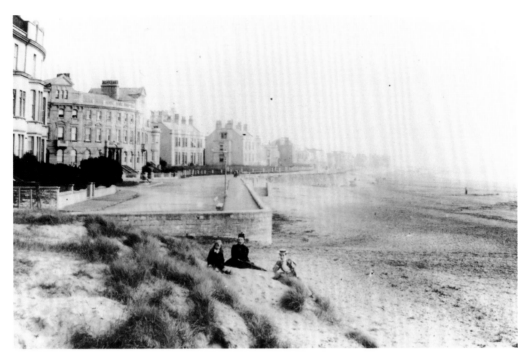

BURNHAM-ON-SEA

It was a lovely afternoon when a small party of us proceeded to Brent Knoll to ramble through the immediate country. Arrived at Brent Knoll we make our way up a dusty lane leading to the village and church, enter the churchyard, and after examining the exterior of the ancient edifice, commence to climb the steep hill familiarly termed the Knoll, determining to reach the summit.

The sun is shining gloriously, and the ascent is no easy task. Yet upward we perseveringly climb, occasionally seeking a change by sitting down for a few minutes in some shady spot, and taking a glance at the lovely scene below us. As BENJAMIN FRANKLIN says, perseverance is bound to bring its own reward, and never more do we realise the truth of this than when we reach with a shout of triumph the top of the Knoll. The scene that lies stretched before us on all sides is surpassingly beautiful, and is a rich reward for any fatigue the ascent has cost us. Old Sol is in one of his happiest moods, and the brilliancy of his smiles adds considerably to the grandeur of the surrounding country. A delightful breeze playing about the top of the hill fans our heated faces, and for some time we stand drinking in the delicious air and admiring the magnificent view before us. The undulating meadow lands in which cattle are quietly grazing, the belts of trees wreathed in foliage of lovely green, the Lilliputian-looking villages, and Burnham sea, with its ceaseless music, sparkling like so many gems in the distance—all this constitutes a scene which is not easily effaced from the memory.

'Time waits for no man' is an old adage, and remembering this we turn our faces towards East Brent, and commence to make a descent, being desirous of paying a visit to Archdeacon DENISON'S place. Just as it is more easy to swim with the tide than against it, so it is easier to make a descent than an ascent, as many only too well know, and needless to say we are not long getting to the bottom of the hill. Then we catch for the first time a good glimpse of the Venerable gentleman's house half hidden in a thick belt of trees, and standing in peaceful serenity within a stone's throw of the church. Having inspected a portion of the grounds we wend our way to the edifice, which, being open, we timidly enter. No service being on, we at once begin examining the interior. One cannot help being struck with the beautiful decorations which meet one's eyes at all points and turns. Banners containing Scriptural texts and quotations from the Common Prayer Book are suspended on the pillars, while similar texts and quotations are also suitably and attractively arranged round the walls. The pulpit is profusely adorned with lovely flowers, and as for the altar, it is brilliantly decorated, and presents a most picturesque appearance.

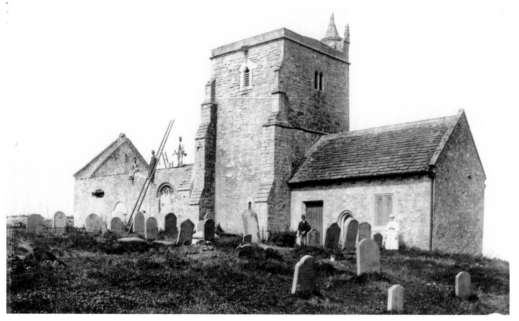

OLD CHURCH, UPHILL

Being informed that a service would be held at half-past six o'clock, at which Archdeacon DENISON would be present, we make up our minds to attend it, and as there is an hour to wait we ramble into the village and utilize the time by partaking of a rural tea. On our return we meet the Archdeacon slowly walking with the aid of a stick up the footpath to the church. After an exchange of a few kindly words we enter the building together, and the tintinnabulation of the bell having ceased, the service commences. The Archdeacon takes the leading part, and the service, though short, is of an impressive character. Notwithstanding that he is something like 85 years of age, Archdeacon DENISON still actively engages himself in church matters, and sets a laudable example to younger men by turning every minute to good account. . ..

And of the Venerable Archdeacon it can conscientiously be said that he is a great husbander of time, using it judiciously and wisely. Rising almost every morning before six o'clock, he turns every hour to good account, replying to his numerous correspondents, studying the Book of books and other theological works, participating every day in devotional services in his little church, and taking out-door exercise. Not unfrequently, too, his well-known face is seen in London and other places, the interests of the Church claiming all his energy, time, money, and talents. How dearly he loves the Church of England, and how much he is concerned for her welfare, may be seen from the

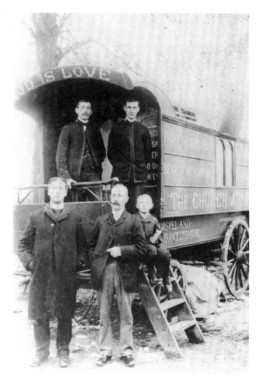

WEDMORE

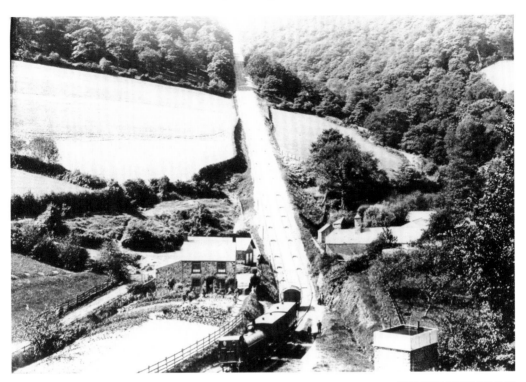

COMBEROW INCLINE

following extract from a letter written by the Venerable Archdeacon to the author of this book: 'All the money that I have to spare—and it is not much—goes in the cause of the Church of England, in the endeavour to recover for her her true constitutional position in Church and State. The position is a "Divine Gift." Like all other "Divine Gifts" it has been invaded and betrayed—invaded from without and betrayed from within. What I have left of life, and strength, and energy, and means, goes in the Church's cause.

Archdeacon DENISON never speaks without revealing a mind of wonderful fertility and vigour, and his utterances, full of weight and earnestness as they are, always command the deepest attention of every thoughtful listener. A powerful and caustic writer on matters affecting Church and State, but a man of gentle disposition and generous sympathies in private life, the Venerable Archdeacon has won the esteem and goodwill of a large circle of persons, and is greatly respected in the Church of England, whose cause he has championed with so much zeal and ability.

But to the church again. The service over, we once more make tracks for the Knoll. The return ramble is most delightful. The heat of the sun has abated, and in its stead has sprung up a soft refreshing breeze, very welcome to us now weary-growing travellers. The Knoll is at last ascended, and after a short rest on the top and another good look at the splendid scene around us, we commence the descent which is safely and quickly made. On arriving in the village we find our horse and trap awaiting us, and most enjoyable is the drive home in the pleasant quiet of eventide.

Charles Press

DIARY OF THE REVD SYDENHAM HERVEY

1872

Easter Sunday. 31st

Collins preached in the morning. I in the afternoon. Crosswell in the evening. Good congregations. 100 communicants altogether, at the two celebrations. Had supper with Crosswell.

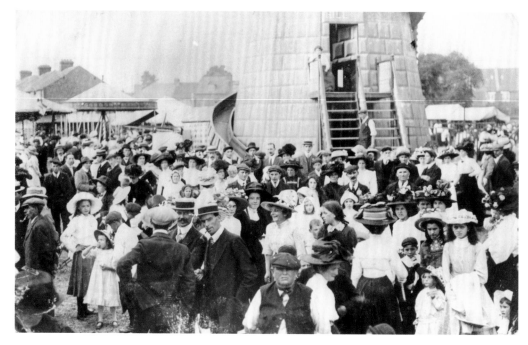

GLASTONBURY TOR FAIR

Monday April 1st

Went to Wells by the 5 o'clock train. All there except John. Intended to have gone back to B[ridg]water for Sunday, but at the last moment was persuaded to stop.

Saturday 6th.

Still at Wells.

Sunday 7th, 1st after Easter

Went to Cathedral in the morning. Fair sermon from Canon Meade. St Cuthbert's in the evening. Good sermon from Beresford, the Vicar.

Monday 8th

Weighed at the Station 10st 6lb.

Wretched day. People arriving all the afternoon. Charley Hoare (bridegroom) [who was to marry the bishop's daughter and the diarist's sister], Walter, William Alfred, Hugh, and Mr and Mrs (Henry) Hoare, brothers—Mr and Mrs William Hoare (uncle), William Oakfield Hoare (cousin) four sisters unmarried, and Mr and Mrs Hallward: Mr and Mrs Strickland. Mrs Kinnaird (aunt), Mr and Mrs Locke King (aunt), Lord Charles and Lady Harriet and Isabel Hervey: Lady Alfred and Mary Hervey; Bristol, Geraldine and Mary: Aunt Minnie Singleton; Pie: Sir Charles and Lady Bunbury. Two young Fletchers: my brother John: Rodney and his sister Patience: George Hervey (cousin), Mr Sparke (lawyer) and Ashington (old Tutor). Most of them had to be lodged about the town. We sat to dinner over forty.

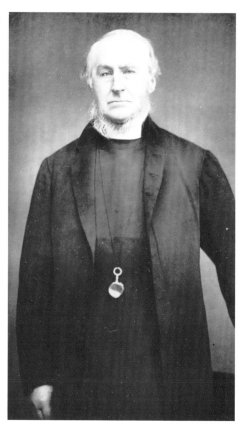

LORD ARTHUR HERVEY,
BISHOP OF BATH AND WELLS

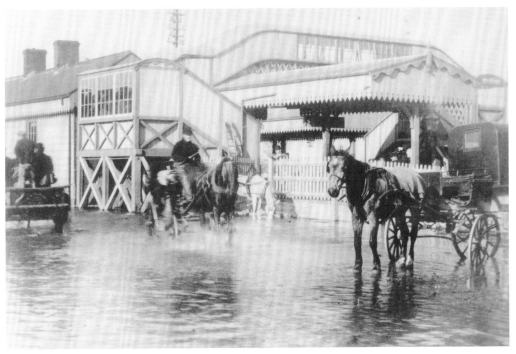

FLOODS, GLASTONBURY

Tuesday 9th

The long expected day come at last. Beautiful weather. I had a two hour's walk before 9 o'clock prayers. Service was at 11.30 punctually.

The choir was filled with people admitted by tickets. The nave was of course free, and a great many people were present. It was a beautiful sight. There were 10 bridesmaids—my 3 sisters—Charley's 4 sisters, Isabel, and Mary Hervey, and Patience Rodney. The bride and bridesmaids, and my father and mother were met at the great W door of the Cathedral by the Dean, choir, and several of the Cathedral clergy, and walked up the nave in procession, singing a hymn. The Dean performed the service, my father, in his robes, giving the bride away. The best man was William Hoare, brother of the bridegroom. Immediately after service was over, two photographs were taken in front of the Palace—one of the brothers and sisters, Herveys and Hoares—the other of all the relations. Then came breakfast—about 160 sat down in the crypt. Bristol proposed the Bride and Bridegroom and Charley returned thanks—Henry Hoare proposed my father and mother—my father returned thanks and proposed the Dean, who replied in a very witty speech. My brother John proposed the bridesmaids, and William Hoare, the best man, returned thanks for them. At about 3 o'clock THEY drove off in a carriage and four to Bath, going on to London by rail that evening. The next morning they were to go on to Dover, and then to Paris on route for Rome.

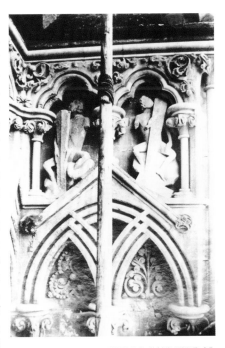

WELLS CATHEDRAL

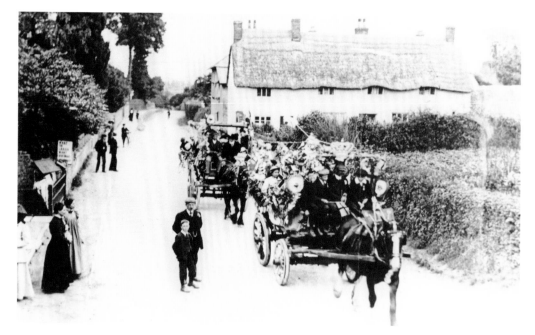

CREECH ST MICHAEL

Our huge party split up into different excursion parties that afternoon. I went to Glastonbury with William, Alfred and Hugh Hoare. We missed the train coming home, and had to take a trap.

In the evening after dinner we had some fireworks in front of the Palace. . .

Sunday 14th, 2nd after Easter

Collins preached in the morning. Crosswell in the afternoon and Evening. I took Union in the afternoon and had service at Dunwear in the evening. Good congregation—sung hymns and a canticle. Went to supper with Crosswell. Very low spirited all day. Reaction, after champagne and excitement of last week.

Sunday October 16th 1898.

I preached my last sermons in Wedmore church. The church was crammed in the evening though a very wet night.

Friday October 21st

There was a tea in the church school room, the room being well filled and beautifully decorated. After tea the seats were re-arranged and the choir and others sang part songs and hymns. In the course of these Mr John Green, Parish Churchwarden, presented me with the parish testimonial, viz. a revolving book case with the Encyclopedia Britannica in 25 volumes, whole morocco, and inscription, and a handsome lamp. Mr Price, Dr Tyley, Messrs J.B. Millard, Singleton, Whish and Pizey all spoke very kindly. I made a very feeble reply. The kindness and feeling shown throughout, in all the arrangements and proceedings, moved me more than I can say. The room was cram full.

Revd Sydenham Hervey

THE JUBILEE CELEBRATIONS IN
THE *WESTERN GAZETTE* DISTRICT
A Specially-compiled Summary.

In no part of the world-wide dominions of our Empress-Queen Victoria was her Diamond jubilee more loyally or enthusiastically celebrated than in the area over which the *Western Gazette* circulates. In the early morn of the ever-memorable June 22nd there issued from almost every tower in town and village throughout

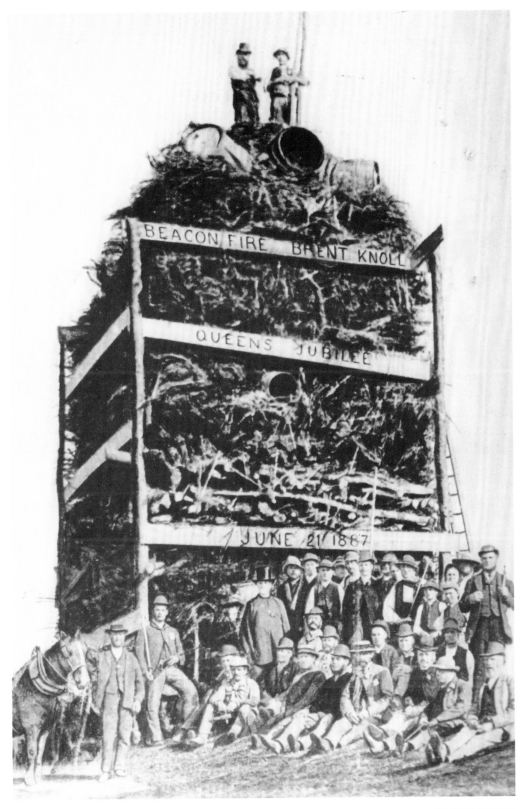

BRENT KNOLL

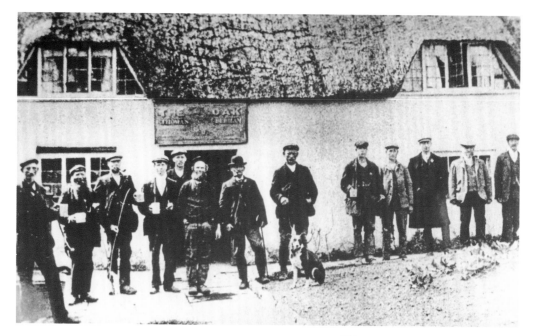

HAYMORE END, NORTH CURRY

the counties of Somerset, Dorset, Wilts, Hants, and Devon, a joyous intimation that the anxiously awaited day had at last dawned; and, later, a summons to render unto the Giver of all Good thanksgiving and praise for a reign which has conferred manifold blessings, not only upon the English speaking race throughout the world, but upon mankind generally. In untold instances these services attracted reverent and overflowing congregations, and in numerous parishes they assumed the form of a united thanksgiving, the parochial clergy and the ministers of the Free Churches jointly conducting. A rejoicing, national or otherwise, would to the average Briton seem somewhat of a pretence without a feast, therefore, in accordance with one of the best observed traditions of our country, the principal item in the programme of the day's festivities in many towns and villages was a dinner, at which 'The Roast Beef of Old England' was the staple joint. Feasting over, the remainder of the day was invariably spent in merry-making and general festivity, and the evening witnessed pyrotechnic displays and illuminations, whilst at ten o'clock there was ignited on scores of hills in the South-west one of those beacon fires, of which some three thousand were arranged in the British Isles, which formed such a unique and interesting feature of the Diamond Jubilee Celebrations.

Western Gazette Almanac, 1898

CELEBRATION OF THE DIAMOND JUBILEE

The great day, when it came, found Bath prepared to show her loyalty to the utmost. To the great majority it was a day of pleasure; to the few, upon whom devolved the work of initiation, it brought with the pleasure a round of unremitting toil, and no Bathonian could have had his powers of endurance put to a greater test than the Mayor. Over and above the power of being ubiquitous, which he displayed in such a marked degree, Mr Woodiwiss showed himself only too anxious to provide 'the sinews of war.' 'It was only right,' said *The Bath Herald*, 'it should be placed on record that with unwonted generosity the Mayor discharged out of his private purse the whole of the cost of the day's proceedings, the citizens not being called upon to contribute one single penny to rejoicings carried out on a far more elaborate scale than on any previous occasion in Bath, and on a scale, too, which eclipsed that undertaken by any other city in the West of England. We believe the Mayor in so generously undertaking to be host on the occasion, was mainly actuated by two reasons. Having already entertained in a very liberal manner those in the city, in a better position in life, he was anxious

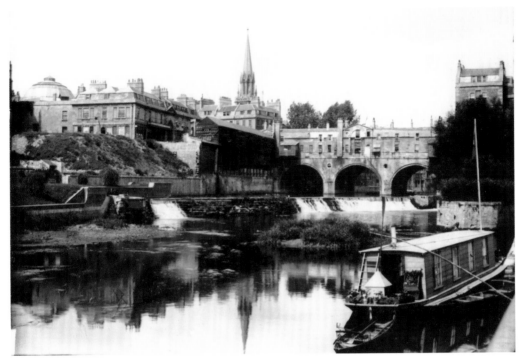

PULTENEY BRIDGE, BATH

that the poorer classes should also partake of his hospitality, and, secondly, by relieving the citizens of all responsibility in the provision of those things which are looked for on a day of public rejoicing, he hoped they would be induced to swell the fund for the establishment of the Art Gallery, a scheme in which he takes the deepest interest and hopes to see well started before the expiration of his term of office. The city is fortunate in having for its Mayor in so memorable a year a gentleman possessed of such public spirit and such marked liberality as Mr George Woodiwiss, a worthy successor to the many energetic and patriotic citizens who have preceded him in the Chief Magistracy.'

The permanent memorial of an Art Gallery destined to be opened by the Duke of Cambridge is dealt with in detail elsewhere, and at this stage, therefore, a passing reference to it must suffice. The scheme was not of course sufficiently advanced to be included in any way in the programme of the day which was as follows:

'6.30 a.m.—A Royal salute of 21 guns in the Royal Victoria Park.

7.00.—The bells of all the various Churches to be rung. It will also be arranged for peals to be rung throughout the day.

10.00.—The Corporation to assemble in the Council Chamber at the Guildhall to vote an Address to Her Majesty.

10.30—Service at the Abbey, to be attended by the Mayor and Corporation in State. The Clergy and Ministers of all Denominations will be invited to attend in their robes, and special seats will be reserved for them.

11.00.—At the conclusion of the Service a civic procession will be formed and, headed by the Volunteer Band, will proceed to Henrietta Park by way of the Market Place, Bridge Street, Pulteney Street, and Sunderland Street. At the Park the City Band will perform, and Mr Farwell, on behalf of Captain Forester, will hand over to the Mayor the title deeds of the Park. The Mayor will then be asked to plant a tree in commemoration of the day, after which the procession will return to the Guildhall by way of Henrietta Street.

8.00 to 12.00—Bullocks will be roasted in the field in front of the Mayor's residence, Hazelwood, Warminster Road; the Association Cricket field, and the Lower Common Recreation Ground.

12.00 to 4.00—Meat will be distributed to the deserving poor and aged in the various districts, to whom

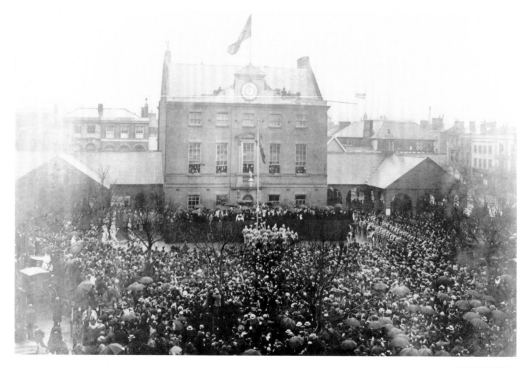

TAUNTON

tickets will have previously been distributed.

1.00 p.m.—Aged People's Dinner at the Drill Hall. It is expected that about 1,500 will be catered for. The dinner will be provided by Messrs Fisher & Co.

2.50.—School children, to the number of 8,000, will assemble in the Royal Avenue, having first had the medals presented by the Mayor distributed at their respective schools. They will then proceed to the Middle Common, where refreshments and entertainments will be provided. The Mayor to plant an oak.

5.30.—Balloon ascent.

6.30.—Variety entertainment.

10.00.—Illumination of Sham Castle, fireworks and bonfires.

The bonfires for which the Committee are responsible are those at Prospect Stile, Claverton Down and Twerton Round Hill.'

Such a programme, it may well be imagined, attracted many visitors to the city, which, under the influence of its holiday garb and a plentitude of sunshine, certainly never looked brighter. The very atmosphere seemed to breathe gaiety. Folks were early astir, and many seemed to think it a positive duty to miss no single item of the celebration, an occupation which kept them well employed from early morning until the sun sank behind the hills and was succeeded by those other fiery orbs which flashed out from every point of vantage up and down the country, the pride of England in Victoria her Queen.

Armistead Cay (ed.)

THE MAYOR'S BANQUET

Some indication of the manner in which Mr Woodiwiss intended to carry out the duties of the mayoralty was afforded on the occasion of the Civic Banquet, when, having determined that the invitation list should be as widely representative as possible, he permitted his hospitality to be bounded only by the limits of the Banqueting Hall. A record civic feast was the result, no less than 220 guests being entertained. Never since the time-honoured custom had been revived by the late Alderman Anthony Hammond, had so large a company

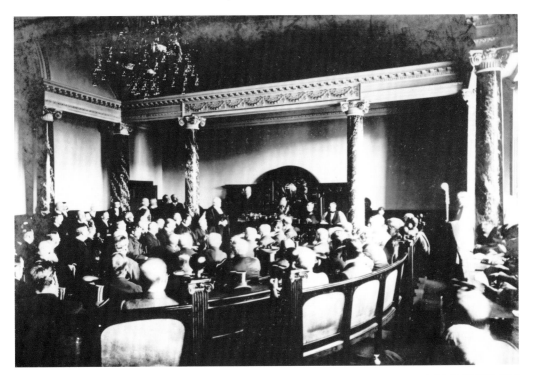

DUKE OF CAMBRIDGE RECEIVES CITY FREEDOM

been catered for. With his customary care in matters of detail, the Mayor had provided every auxiliary likely to secure the happiness of his guests. The floral decorations, selected and arranged with a view to the preservation of an artistic scheme of colouring, were voted especially charming. Brilliantly illuminated, and crowded in every part with the long tables, each loaded with everything which could appeal to both eye and taste, the Banqueting Hall looked truly inviting.

The following was the menu:

Native Oysters   Anchovies

Clear Turtle   Thick Turtle

Turbot, Sauce Hollandaise   Fried Smelts

Sweetbreads larded   Sauce Supreme

Compote of Pigeons en bordure

Boiled Turkey Bechamel   Ox Tongues

Saddle Mutton   Ham in Champagne

Pheasants   Golden Plover

Cocoanut Pudding

Maraschino Jelly   Queen Mab's Cream

Mince Pies   Cheese Straws

Iced Nesselrode Pudding

Dessert

During the evening a pleasant selection of music was contributed by the Rhine String Band, the programme also including songs by Mr Starkey Baxter and Mr C.E. Poole. It was a reign of hospitality on a refined and generous scale, which augured well indeed for coming events.

Armistead Cay (ed.)

ADDITIONAL HONOURS FOR THE MAYOR

The honour of being, for however brief a period, Citizen Number One of no mean city, and of earning innumerable friendships without making a single enemy, was felt by Mr Woodiwiss to be an honour indeed. He certainly desired no greater one. It could not be said of him that he ever courted place or authority; yet the mayoralty had been pressed upon him, and during his regime many unexpected distinctions were destined to follow. To the magnificent citizens' presentation we have allotted a separate section. It was announced in December that the Lord Chancellor had elevated Mr Woodiwiss to the dignity of city magistrate. The following gentlemen were also placed on the Commission of the Peace for the city of Bath at the same time: Major Simpson, Mr James Colmer, and Mr Samuel George Mitchell. Mr Woodiwiss had acted as justice of the Peace on the County Bench for some years. In May we find him declining to fill the aldermanic vacancy, caused by the death of the late Alderman Bright. On returning from Eastbourne, where he had taken a well-earned rest from civic responsibilities, the Mayor received the following letter from the Home Secretary, Sir Matthew White Ridley:

Whitehall; 7th September, 1897.

Sir,—I have received the Queen's commands to transmit to you the accompanying medal, which Her Majesty has been graciously pleased to confer upon you on the completion of the 60th year of her reign. I have to request that you will be good enough to send me an acknowledgement of the receipt of this decoration.

I am, sir, your obedient servant,

M. W. RIDLEY

The Mayor of the City of Bath.

The medal was enclosed in an red Morocco case, bearing on the outside an Imperial crown and the dates 1837-1897. A similar decoration was conferred upon the Chief Magistrates throughout the country, and it is now so well-known as scarcely to need description. It is of oxydised silver, lozenge-shaped, and attached to

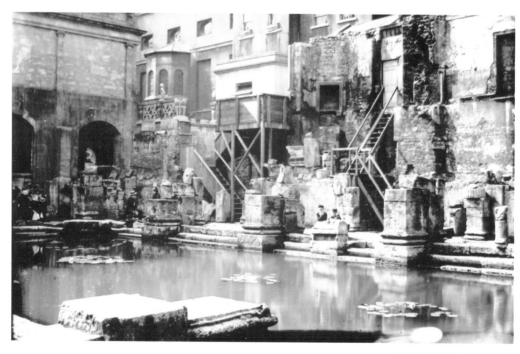

ROMAN BATHS, BATH

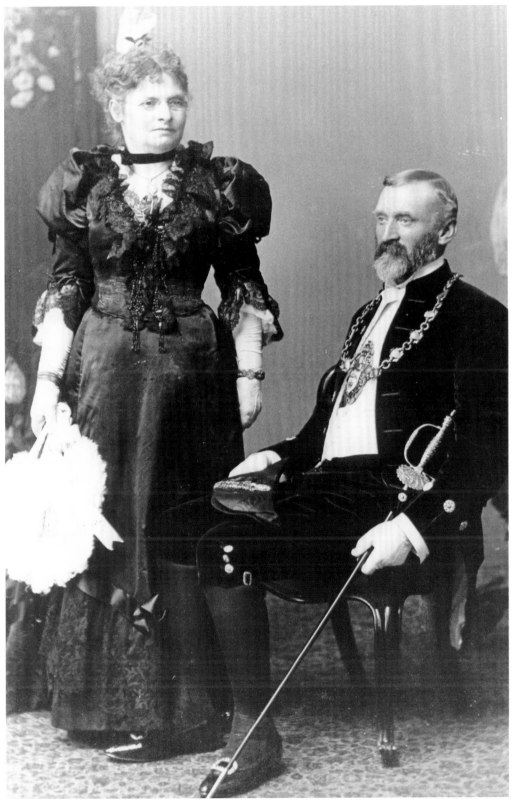

ALDERMAN & MRS W. LOCK, MAYOR AND MAYORESS OF TAUNTON

a ribbon in two shades of blue, with a silver bar. On each side is a bust of Her Majesty, Queen Victoria, one representing her as she appeared in 1837, and the other fashioned after the coinage design by Sir Edgar Boehm. Accompanying the earlier portrait are the words, `Longitudo dierum in dextera eius et in sinistra gloria:' and at the sides of the later portrait, `Victoria annum regni Sexagesimum feliciter claudit. XX. IVN. MDCCCXCVII.' Mr Woodiwiss had also the distinguished honour of being presented to Her Majesty at Buckingham palace. He was present at the Reception and Ball given in July by the Corporation of London in commemoration of the Queen's Diamond jubilee—one of the most brilliant functions of the century, for which between five and six thousand invitations were issued. The Town Clerk (Mr John Stone) was also present. Both these gentlemen were among the computed million onlookers at the Royal Naval Review at Spithead, having been invited with many other Mayors and Town Clerks in the West of England by the Great Western Railway Company, to view the spectacle from the steamship Roebuck. In October the Mayor, who was accompanied by the Mayoress, was among the 199 English Mayors and

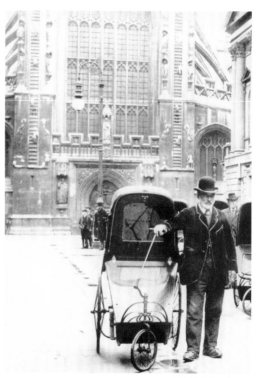

BATH CHAIRS

Mayoresses at the Mansion House Ball given by the Lord Mayor of London and the Lady Mayoress.

On the Monday evening following the citizens' presentation the Mayor was entertained at a complimentary dinner at Messrs Fortt's, Milsom Street. The chair was filled by Mr Alderman Ruble, who was supported by the Revd Canon Quirk and about 60 representative citizens. The 'Health of the Guest of the Evening,' was proposed in cordial terms by the Chairman, and was drunk with enthusiasm. Mr Woodiwiss suitably acknowledged the honour done him.

At the close of the mayoralty, Colonel Arnoll Davis, Chairman of the Pleasure Grounds Committee, invited the Mayor and the other members of the Committee to a luncheon at Messrs Fortt's restaurant. The opportunity was taken of presenting to Mr Woodiwiss the garden spade with which he planted the commemorative oak in Henrietta Park, and also that in the Royal Victoria Park. This was adorned with a silver plate bearing the inscription 'Wielded by George Woodiwiss, Esq., Mayor of Bath. I planted an oak in Henrietta Park on the 22nd of June, 1897. Floreat Bathon et quercus robur.' All inscription round the handle drew attention to the purpose for which the spade had been used at the Royal Victoria Park.

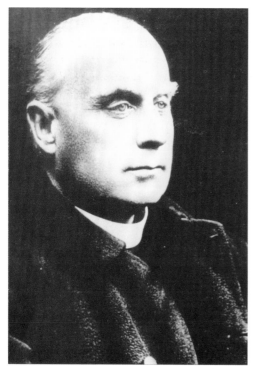

THE REVD V.S.S. COLES,
SHEPTON BEAUCHAMP

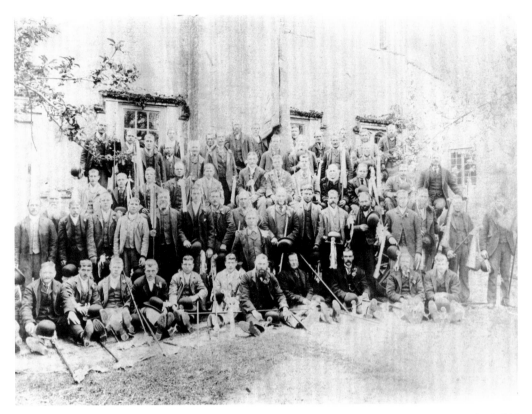

CLUB DAY, STOKE SUB HAMDON

In November the gratifying intimation was conveyed to Mr Woodiwiss that the Earl of Cork had appointed him a Deputy-Lieutenant for the Western division of the County. The other Deputy-Lieutenants for the division are Earl Temple, Mr H. D. Skrine and Mr E.T.D. Foxcroft. The Mayor's regime was drawing rapidly to a conclusion, and it is, perhaps, scarcely necessary to say that the news of this high distinction conferred upon him, gave the greatest satisfaction to the citizens, who were themselves spontaneously uniting at the time, to present him with a tangible earnest of their goodwill and their appreciation of services loyally rendered.

A very valuable souvenir of the mayoralty was the illuminated address presented to Mr Woodiwiss by the City Council in November. The text of the address was as follows:

CITY OF BATH.

At a meeting of the Council of the City of Bath held at the Guildhall in the said City, on Tuesday, the 9th day of November, 1897, under the presidency of Major Charles Simpson, JP, Mayor, it was resolved unanimously, upon the motion of Mr Alderman Chaffin, seconded by Mr Councillor Farwell, that the very cordial thanks of this Council be and they are hereby given to George Woodiwiss, Esq., JP, DL, the retiring Mayor, for the ability, courtesy, efficiency, and marked munificence with which he has discharged the duties of the mayoralty during the past year.

Chas. H. Simpson, Mayor
John Stone, Town Clerk

At the head of the address appeared the Arms of the City and Mr Woodiwiss's crest.

Armistead Cay (ed.)

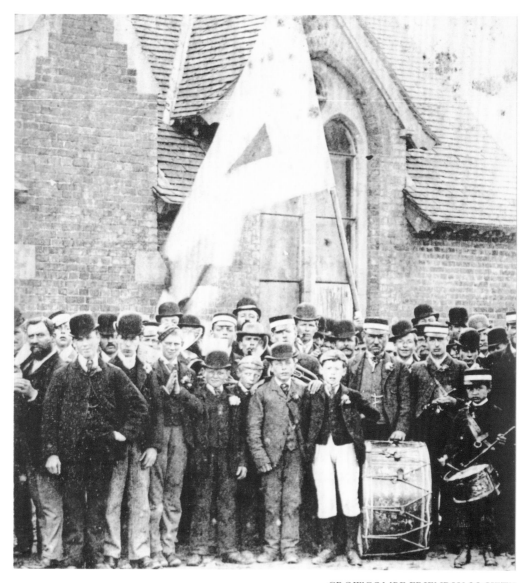

CROWCOMBE FRIENDLY SOCIETY

TOMMY NUTTY'S CLUB FEAST DAY

Ov all the whole yeer round, dye know, the girtest, grandest day,
Amongst us zimple conntry voak, is Twenty-ninth of May.
Ther's harvest whoam an Christmus time, but taint no good to talk,
The grandest day as we do know, is when our Club do walk.
The womin voaks be up thic marn avore the cocks do crow,
To git ther wark all done avore the Club goo round you know,
Vor bless 'ee tis a purty zight to zee us in our glory,
Wi our musickers an purty vlags—but ther I'm vore my ztory!
Now vust of all as you med note, as thof to gi us warning,
The ringers zet the bells agwine, at vive o'clock in the marning.
We'm purty dapper arter that—doant lose much time be sure,
Ther's vlags to vly, and oaken boughs to plant at every door.

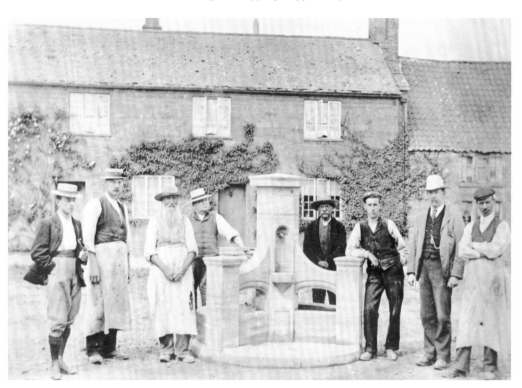

MONTACUTE

An strings ov vlowers an evergreens to hang athirt the ztreet,
I'd like ee jist to zee it once, I ashure ee tis a treat.
Well we work away wi might an main, that's the way to come it,
Till breakfust time then doant stop long, jist catch a bit ov summit.
Then off we goes each one to dress, to dress all in his best,
Wi clothes all birshed, an tutty pinned zo nicely in each vest.
But zummit comes athirt my heart, an brings a vew hot tears,
As I don the hat poor Vather wore to Club so many year:
I needs must think ov him once more, wi his dear old happy veace,
How proud he war ov Club day too a mearching in his pleace.
Then Zally kissing off the tears ses her Tommy looks quite zmart.
An I kiss her back agen, I do—Lar bless her little heart!
Then off I goos an meet the rest, an answer to my neame,
As one by one we hear em called, each one does the zame.
We then vall in our pleaces an varm in twos an twos,
Every man's zupposed to walk, or be vined if he revuse.
But I be rather honored like, my post is zummit grand,
They let me carry a purty vlag, an march in vront the band!
Then when each one is in his pleace, wi club ztaff in his hand,
I gets em ready vor to ztart—ov coorse I'm in command:
Then all the vlags be zoon unvurled, zays I 'My lads now come,
An the musickers get ready an then bang goos the drum.
Zo off we ztarts upon our round, ov coorse I leads the way,
An the party musickers ztrike up 'The merry month ov May.'

W. Cook

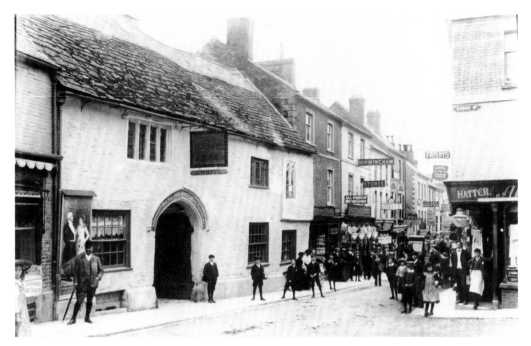

YEOVIL

PLAYING IN THE GALLERY

The interior of Montacute House stirred my imagination—the armoury for example, with helmets and cuirasses used at the time of the Great Rebellion. Whenever I passed through this high square-shaped room I experienced a kind of Ivanhoe romance, and although the Phelips family came into prominence after the Wars of the Roses, echoes from the days of medieval chivalry would be clearly audible to me as I looked up at the weapon-hung walls of the civil antechamber. The main stairway was exciting also, the long stone slabs worn uneven by so much Phelips shoe leather; but most wonderful of all it was to step suddenly into the immense gallery that stretched one hundred and eighty feet from end to end of the house.

How the lonely memories of the old gallery would be scattered, as, with the careless voices of living children, we burst in upon its emptiness; and how hollow, how resonant, its bare boards would sound as our quick feet went pattering, racing down them, unheedful of anything but the impinging actuality of our moment's holiday! How swiftly, too, on a rainy afternoon the time would go by in so spacious a playing room! The great rocking-horse was kept there, the highest-stepping dapple grey ever built by a carpenter, left alone through so many long hours to contemplate with the painted eye the procrastinating twilights of the morning and evening shading their way through sixteen windows, along the coved ceiling of this vast Elizabethan corridor.

The rain would beat against one or other of the high oriel windows at each end of the gallery, where, to the south, the village was overlooked, or where, at the other end, the stately ornamental North Gardens could be seen, with their dark drenched yew trees standing like royal sentinels against the meadows that rose into view beyond the privileged enclosure.

Llewelyn Powys

MRS PHELIPS

I do not think I have ever seen an old lady with so delicate a complexion. Even in her great age the poise of her head was light and graceful as a rose upon its stalk. The moulding of her skull was as fragile as that of the most precious porcelain and there was a flush upon her cheeks that reminded me of the inside of some of the sea shells in my father's cabinet. Her head was as ethereal in appearance as was Shelley's head, and she was, as a matter of fact, the daughter of Shelley's cousin, and the poet's first love, the same who forsook him

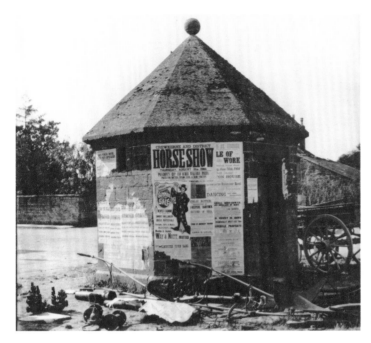

KINGSBURY EPISCOPI

to bestow the favours of her beauty upon the wealthy Squire of Coker Court in Somerset.

When old Nancy and her daughter would, with crooked spines, be 'sticking' under the great Montacute sycamores, crooning to each other on the eternal subjects of back and belly, this little light-footed great lady could be seen walking along the drive that ran under the avenue to Galpin's Lodge; unless she had chosen, as she sometimes did, the damp woodland path of Park Cover, a woodland path bordered by a shelving bank thick with mosses out of which in the autumn slippery toadstools of bright scarlet would grow. Who ever knew the long, long thoughts that were revolving in that solitary old woman's head, so aristocratic and so ancient, as she trod the ancestral woods of her husband's family, which, during those mild wet months before Christmas, never ceased from their melancholy dripping?. . .

One of my earliest recollections of Mrs Phelips, senior, is of her driving me and her grandson Gerard, who was my own age, to Yeovil. Arrived in the town, she told the coachman to draw up at the toy-shop which stood opposite 'The Choughs.' On the proprietor's obsequiously hurrying out to the carriage door, he was instructed to give us our choice of all his wares. I was so bewildered as I was ushered round the crowded passages of the small shop that I selected a painted tricycle that went by clockwork, afterward envying the cooler judgement of my companion, who brought back for our inspection in the gallery a very expensive, and apparently inexhaustible, conjuring box.

Llewelyn Powys

WASSAILING

High up towards the head of the oldest tree hangs a thick bush, fresh in leaf and covered with white berries that look like pearls.

That is the mistletoe.

It is quite plentiful in Somerset in all the orchards by the moors. The missel-thrush—holm-screech we call him, because of his voice, and because he loves the holly as well—devours the berries, which are filled with a sticky substance, so that the seeds cling to his beak. 'He do clean the beak o' un,' as we say, against a branch, and now and again in some crevice of the bark a seed sticks fast, out of the reach of weather and rain. It throws out roots, and at last thrives into a good big bough, until some Christmas-time the folk come out from house and cut it down to hang up from the dark oaken kitchen beam.

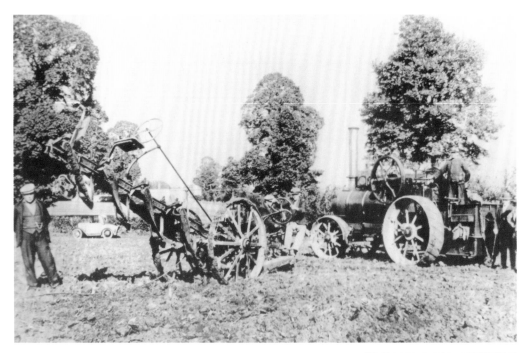

STEAM PLOUGH, BUTLEIGH

Then there is a party— 'no fear!' The crowder works his fiddlestick. He of the hobnails dances by the hour. The maid of the broken staves blushes a refusal, but at last sings the old song in full with pride. She of the shrill voice, that sounded so shrewd about the work, bustles around the hearth all smiles, cooing a welcome to each guest in turn, and hoping 'sure! that everybody have a-got all they do want.'

The good old orchard has done its best to keep their spirits up. For the two-handled cider-cup goes round with a toast and a drop o' gin in it. In days gone by upon Old Christmas Eve they used to all go out and set up the toast in the fork of the best apple-tree, and then they shouted till they were hoarse:

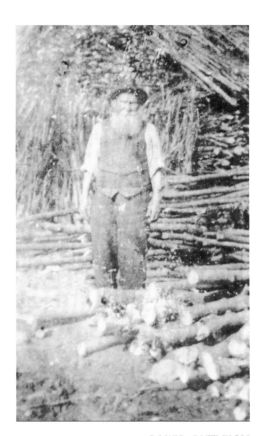

> Apple-tree, apple-tree,
> I do wassail thee,
> To blow an' to bear
> Hat-vulls, cap-vulls,
> An' dree-bushel-bags-vull,
> An' my pockets vull too.
> Hoorah!

But nobody thinks nowadays of wassailing the orchards. We only drink 'good-luck!' as we sit and roast by a great wood fire, and there is an end to it.

Walter Raymond

BAKER, BUTLEIGH

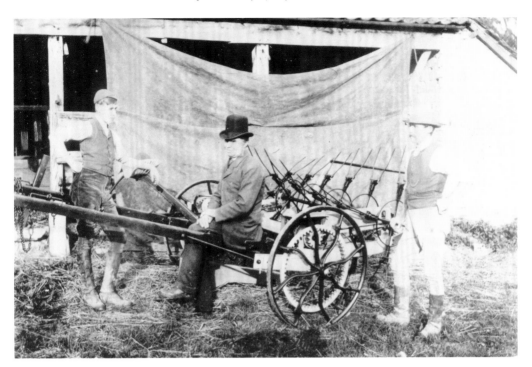

HAYMAKER

CIDER

One great difficulty with the peasants in Somersetshire is what is called 'the cider question.' This county being one of the finest cider-producing counties in England, the system prevails of giving the labourers daily, in small kegs or firkins, a certain quantity of cider, varying in different districts, but seldom less, I believe, than three pints per day. I obtained the testimony of an old man, who has had fifty years' experience as a farm labourer, and he gave me a truthful description of the horrible liquor that is given to the agricultural labourer under the ironical name of cider. It is a well-known fact that in Somersetshire, and in other of the western cider-producing counties, the farmer nearly always keeps 'two taps running,' according to the expression of that part of the country: one tap for himself and his friends, and one tap for the farm labourers. The farmer's own cider—I can speak from my own knowledge as well as from the evidence of my information—is most carefully made. The very best apples are selected, and the manufacturing process is carefully gone through, and real cider is produced. If a stranger to the country wants to taste the best cider, the farmer will give him what he will tell him in confidence that he keeps for his 'own drinking.' Now for the labourers' cider-tap number two. The very worst apples are, in the first place, selected—the 'windfalls'; and these, with dirt and slugs, are ground up for the peasants. When the 'windfalls' are used for feeding the pigs the labourer has what is called the 'second wringing'—that is to say, the apples for the farmer's 'own drinking' cider are put into the press, and after the best part of the juice has been extracted the cider 'cheese,' as the mass of apples in the press is called, is subjected to yet greater pressure, and what is expressed from the 'cheese' on this occasion is called the 'second wringing.' This is greatly inferior to the 'first wringing.' To complete the process and make a liquor worthy of tap number two, the following plan is adopted: To every hogshead of the 'second wringing' is added four gallons of hop-water. This is added for the purpose of preserving the 'second wringing,' which without such addition would, from its thinness and inferiority, turn to vinegar. My informant, to give me some idea of the difference in quality between the farmer's 'two taps,' said that good cider usually costs about 30s. a hogshead, whilst the 'second wringing' was worth only about 10s. a hogshead.

There is no doubt that the cider system is a very bad one. It would be infinitely better that the peasant should have the value of the cider—which, by the bye, is generally estimated by the farmer to be worth considerably more than it is really worth—in money. To a man with such wretched wages every penny is of value. But the

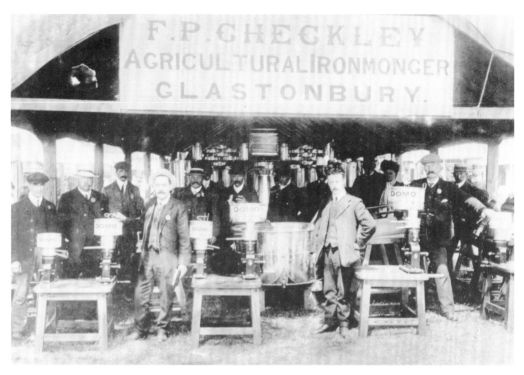

AGRICULTURAL MERCHANT

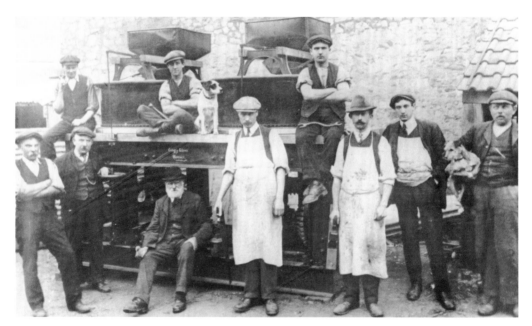

MILLWRIGHTS, WATCHET

system is unfair to the labourer, because under the 'cider system' his wages are greatly overestimated; and I believe the horrible compound which the farmers call cider, but which I think should properly be called vinegar, works the most pernicious effects upon the constitution of the rural labourer.

F. G. Heath

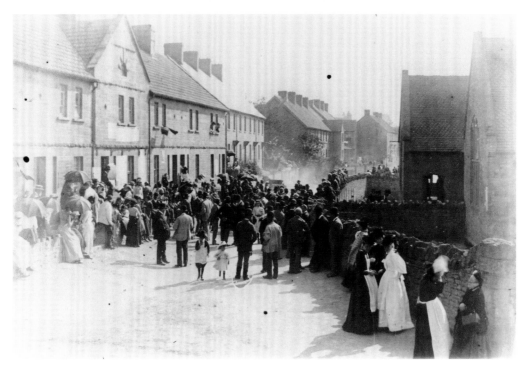

ELECTION TIME, STOKE SUB HAMDON

COUNTY COUNCIL CANVASSING ETC. (1904)

We have heard so much and told so much of recent experience in connection with the above that we feel a considerable diffidence in committing anything further on the subject to Album paper. We bespeak the kind inattention of those to whom a thrice-told tale may well prove wearisome.

Finding that the big battalions were chiefly at the disposal of the Clatterbark Candidate, and wishing naturally to cut as large a figure ourselves as might be possible, we joined the Clogumber forces in the Puddleton division, giving our special attention to the neighbouring village of Humpty Dumpty.

Canvassing is a task to which we have always had a particular aversion, chiefly, no doubt, because as a rule we have been in the way of receiving more rebuffs than encouragement.

We therefore began our campaign with great diffidence and nervousness, spending much time overlooking the prize cocks and hens belonging to our principal supporter, and in going through the lists of voters with him and noting down the age, health and religious persuasion of each. At the present juncture, this latter information was especially required, as it was, of course, most important to find out whether the Education Act was to be stormed by an open breach in the walls by the battering ram of Passive Resistance, or undermined by hints of increases in the rates.

So we passed away the earlier hours of the afternoon in the procrastinating manner of one who has an appointment with the dentist and lingers at each shop window by the way in the hope of finding excuses to put off the evil hour.

And indeed, the pleasant cottage house was a place to tempt one to linger. Spotless within and without, comfort and thrift and intelligence seemed to shine from its very walls, and the active sympathy and cooperation of the heads of the household in all good things filled one with a happiness quite impossible to put into words.

We are often tempted to despond when thinking over the social conditions of our time, but when in a house of this type one sees what is possible to people with artisan wages only, given character, wide interests, thrift and love, one may surely take hope again.

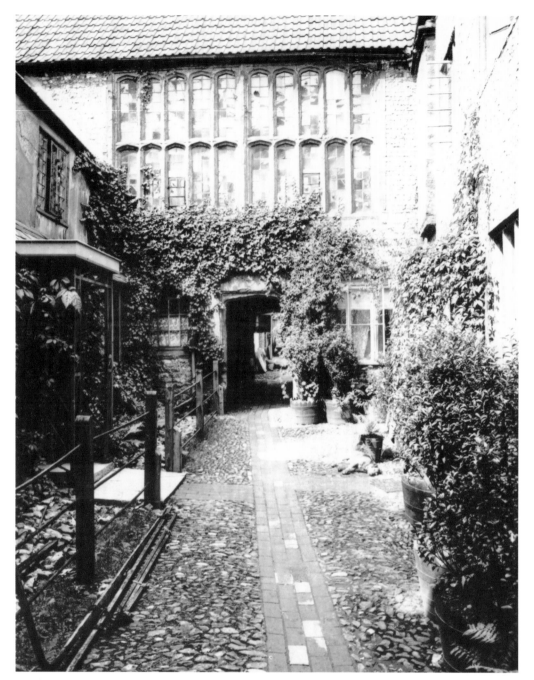

CHARD

But away with lingering, and to our canvass. How nervously and stutteringly we began, and how we rejoiced at finding the first voter out, and how eloquent with constant practice and reiteration we finally became. So much so that the iron tongue and the brazen throat in the classical quotation would have been an invaluable aid.

We found ourselves completely in the atmosphere of Walter Raymond's stories, and as we mouthed our parts upon the little stage, almost every one of his characters would at one time or another take part in the dialogue with us.

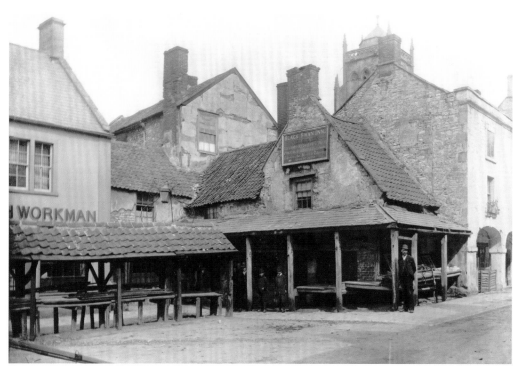

BLACK SWAN, SHEPTON MALLET

Sometimes, indeed, the veil would be briefly lifted and some darkly hinted tragedy would be drawn for us, such as Thomas Hardy would love to elaborate, but for the most part light comedy, we felt, was our true metier, and we skated lightly over the thin ice when it came.

It was at our first call that we met with some criticism on the County Council system of technical instruction. The Voter was out, but an elderly man who was trimming up the hedge proved to be his father, and on learning our errand he began: 'There's one thing about the County Council I can't never see no sense in; they do send a veller round theäse way fer to tich volk how to meäke ther vowels lay when they bain't minded to; fullishness, I do call, I should zim volk as do kip vowels ud know better how to make 'em lay than any veller they could zend hround. I'll tell 'ee what I do do wi' mine when they won't lay—cut ther bloody heads off, that's what I do do wi' 'em—that do soon tich em'.

The old story of an ounce of experience.

It was with some hesitation that we entered the wide portal of the Hare & Hounds to solicit the vote of the landlady, the widow White. Finding her in her very spotless cellar drawing a two-handled mug-full from a barrel, we at once opened the subject, thinking to do our duty and get away quickly. We were cut short with a long volley of fluent utterance. 'No, I han't never a-voted yet an I shouldn't begin now. My Husband, now he used to vote but ther, he've a-bin dead theäse years, poor soul, an I han't never took it on. I do always say ther's a plenty of men to do it, an if they do like it, why, let 'em says I. No, no! Tain't no use, I han't never done it and I shan't never do it, and I've a-promised myself I shouldn't never vote, and I should be wicked if I were to break my promise, now shouldn't I?' We endeavoured to point out what a loss in intelligence and knowledge of the world this represented to the village—but in vain.

'Law now, you do know how to het it up, doan't ee, but Betsy White have a-made up her mind. I shan't vote, but now you be here, why don't ee goo in ther—ther's dree or vour o' they men as have got votes if they do know how to use 'em, and you'll save yourself a tidy step if you do catch 'em here.' Thoughts of the needless frequenting of taverns and other public houses came to our minds, thoughts which it would soon be our duty to be suggesting to others in reading the General Advices on a First Day morning; but we also thought of the interesting and profitable occasion which our Great Founder had with the young men in the

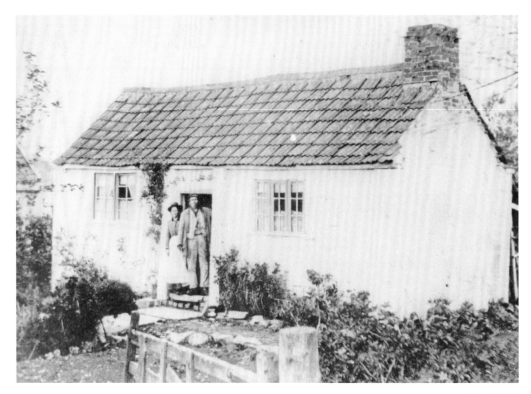

ASHCOTT

tavern, and so we went in to the Inn kitchen, nothing doubting. Seating ourselves in the great open chimney corner by a log fire, we found opposite to us our specialist in the treatment of unwilling egg layers. We called for tea, which was very nicely served, and during a cheerful and convivial hour we have reason to believe that we gained some five votes.

A more spotlessly neat and orderly house we have never seen, a lesson to many temperance houses. The good woman is a noted tyrant in the matter of cleanliness and order, and I was told that 'John Fox Gooden he wer in ther and zeed a brand a-vollen out o' vier, and put en back wi' es stick and she becalled en so for poking the vier, he han't never bin ther, since'.

The end of the evening brought us to a remote habitation in the middle of Sedgemoor—mud-built and one-storied. Two steps down led us into the living room, and the owner came forward to meet us. He was seated on a bench with a wooden chair before him, and on it a lamp and a large heap of freshly-killed moles. Their fore-paws had all been cut off ready for skinning, which operation was in full swing.

Settling down to a chat in the chimney corner, we presently learned more of the ways of 'wants' than we had ever had opportunity to do before. We were shown the home-made wooden traps, with a little loose peg fitted into the middle part. 'Now that's what we do call the muggle pin, and that's because when the want do go droo the trap, he'rn bound to muggly wi' thic ther little pin, and that do get the trap and catch en by the wast and zo we do call en the muggle pin.' He said there was no cruelty in the traps: 'Wants is wonderful quick things to die.' Our friend was a quaint little elderly man, very spry and bright and alert. A pleasant young son and daughter were living with him. His wife, Bessy, had been some years dead. 'Ees, we had vowerteen childer atween us, and I han't never zim'd I could marry no-one else, tho' (a chuckle) 'ther's two or dree o 'em as ud like to hrun up agin me if they could, d'y' know.'

We were hospitably fed with good home-made bread made of wholemeal ground from their own corn at the Puddleton Mill and baked in their own great oven on wood ashes. 'Ees', he reminisced, 'the childer mid have poor cloathes, but they never knew what 'twer to want good bread and butter, nit good shoes to ther vit, and that's two very good things, a good belly full o' victuals and good shoes to kip out the wet, an' I'll tell 'ee another good think, and that's a good vire on the vloor. Ees, that's dree very good things—a good belly-vull o' victuals, and good shoes to yer vit, and a good vier o' 'ood in the chimbley.'

'Tis a wold house, but 'twill last my time, but they don't never do nothen to ut. I do pay the Lard vive pound a year fer theäse wold place.' Two visits an hour, and sometimes not so many, were all we could pay, so much of human interest did we find to detain us.

On another occasion we found only the wife of the voter at home—an elderly and disappointed lady who had come to the conclusion that 'votin' were no good to nobody. Just look at the gouts, now, they be wuss stopped up to year than ever they were. I've a-thought ut all over, and I've a-decided that Joseph shan't go to vote no mwore.' Fortunately we were able in time to dislodge the objection and obtain permission for Joseph to go. 'One time I were a hregler one fer the meetins when my sight were good. I did use to like 'em, and once down to Farmer who-is-it's barn I held up a bit o'yaller peaper to show 'em the colours, and 'twer advertised on the peaper that a woman of size had

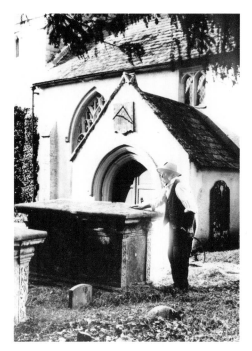

BADGWORTH

a-showed up the colours (a sigh), and so I wer in them days, dy' know, but I've a-bin bad thease six years and t' have a-vetched I away wonderful.'

In almost all the houses we found real comfort, care and thrift, and in spite of buildings old and tumbling down, suffering from the neglect of an absentee landlord, the houses were almost invariably snug and pleasant to be in, and neatly and cleanly kept.

A few weeks have passed since the election day with its exultant victory and once more we find ourselves at the pleasant cottage where we had received so much true hospitality.

A cruel blow has fallen upon the household. After only a few days' illness, the mother is lying dead in the upper room, and the relatives and friends are gathered in their heavy black garments of mourning for the funeral. It is a long walk to the Church, and the day is wild and stormy. The grief-stricken husband, looking pathetically boyish and young, follows the coffin with the elder boy and girl in either hand—attractive children whose beautiful behaviour and helpful ways had shown us in our previous visits what a mother they had had. The little girl of three was taken up in the cart and

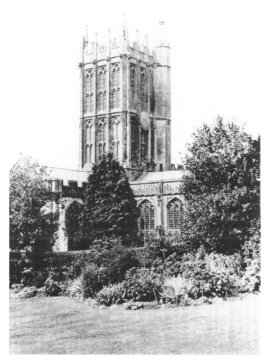

ILMINSTER CHURCH

mercifully dropped to sleep, still asking for the mother she would never see again.

The quiet, restful service in the old church, with a hymn of love and hope, seemed a helpful interlude between the long, stormy walk and the last sad gathering by the grave itself. Here the storm had passed, and there was a gentle radiance over the low soft landscapes stretching away between the hills before us and behind us. Our silent prayer that a like inward peace might somehow come to these so sorely bereaved ones perhaps enabled us in a fuller sense than usual to share with them the feeling of inspiration bequeathed by so noble and so unselfish a life.

Roger Clark

AUDREY

By a mossy bank a little girl—a miniature Audrey—stout, rosy, and ragged, stood with a yellow straw hat aslant on her yellow hair, eating the leaves from a spray of beech in her hand. Audrey looked at us, eating the beech leaves steadily, but would not answer, not even, 'Where's your father to?' For in Somerset the 'to' is put last, and must never be omitted; thus, instead of saying 'I bought this at Taunton,' it is correct to say 'I bought this to Taunton.' There are models under glass cases in places of entertainment with a notice to say that if a penny be inserted the machine will go. Audrey the Little would not speak, but when a penny was put in her hand she began to move, and made off for home with the treasure.

Richard Jefferies

AN ARTIST'S INSPIRATION

Through green fields, in which the grass was rising high and sweet, a footpath took me by a solitary mill with an undershot wheel. The sheds about here are often supported on round columns of stone. Beyond the mill is a pleasant meadow, quiet, still, and sunlit; buttercup, sorrel, and daisy flowered among the grasses down to the streamlet where comfrey, with white and pink-lined bells, stood at the water's edge. A renowned painter, [Frederick] Walker, who died early, used to work in this meadow; the original scene from which he took his picture of The Plough is not far distant. The painter is gone; the grasses and the

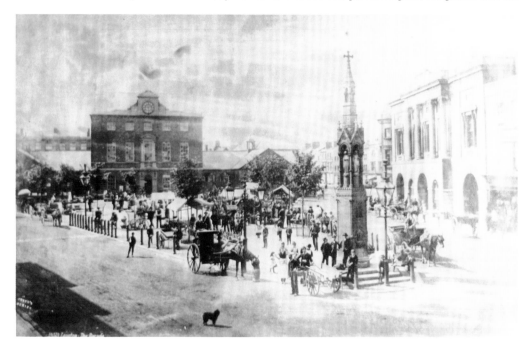

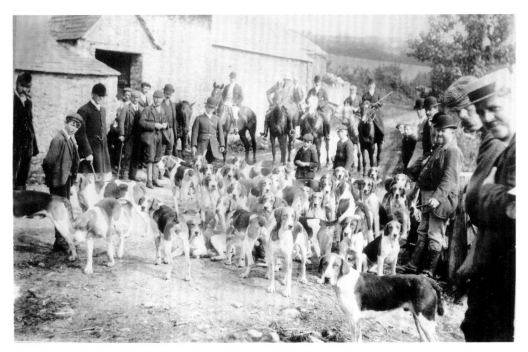

STAGHOUNDS, STAWLEY

flowers are renewed with the summer. As I stood by the brook a water-rat came swimming, drawing a large dock-leaf in his mouth; seeing me, he dived, and took the leaf with him under water.

Richard Jefferies

SELWORTHY

At Selworthy a footpath leads up through a wood on Selworthy hill, and as it ascends, always at the side of the slope, gradually opens out what is perhaps the finest view of Dunkery Beacon, the Dunkery range, and that edge of Exmoor on the shore of the sea. Across a deep vale the Exmoor mountains rise and reach on either hand, immense breadths of dark heather, deep coombes filled with black shadow, and rounded masses that look dry and heated. To the right is the gleaming sea, and the distant sound of the surge comes up to the wood. The headland and its three curves boldly project into the sunlit waters; from its foot many a gallant stag hard pressed by the hounds has swum out into the track of passing vessels. Selworthy woods were still in the afternoon heat; except for the occasional rustle of a rabbit or of a pheasant, there was no evidence of life; the sound of the sea was faint and soon lost among the ferns. Slowly, very slowly, great Dunkery grew less hard of aspect, shadows drew along at the base, while again the declining sun from time to time sent his beams into valleys till now dark. The thatched house at Holnicote by the foot of Selworthy much interested me; it is one of the last of thatched houses inhabited by a gentleman and landed proprietor. Sir Thomas Acland who resides here is a very large owner. Thatch prevails on his estates; thatched cottages, thatched farmhouses, and his thatched mansion. In the coolness of the evening the birds began to sing and squirrels played across the lawn in front of Holnicote House. Humble-bees hummed in the grass and visited the flowers of the holly bushes. Thrushes sang, and chaffinches, and, sweetest of all, if simplest in notes, the greenfinches talked and courted in the trees. Two cuckoos called in different directions, wood-pigeons raised their voices in Selworthy wood, and rooks went over cawing in their deliberate way. In the level meadow from among the tall grasses and white-flowering wild parsley a landrail called 'crake, crake,' ceaselessly. There was a sense of rest and quiet, and with it a joyousness of bird life, such as should be about an English homestead.

Richard Jefferies

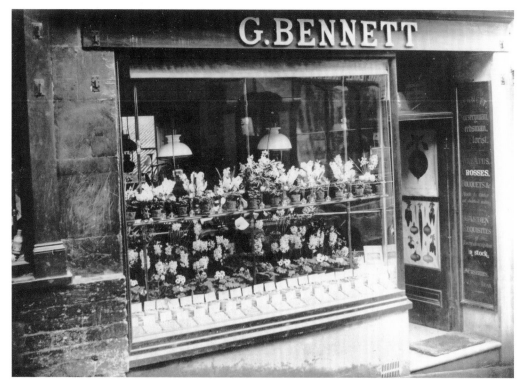

FLORISTS, FROME

MISS SPARKES' PARROT

Miss Sparkes had a maid called Emma. I never observed, however, that she was allowed to play a very active part in the salesmanship of the shop. She was a humble little woman, born, so it seemed, to receive with a silent and saintly patience hasty rebukes for petty errors, petty inaccuracies, and for leaving undone what she ought to have done. Besides Emma this small establishment maintained one other inmate—Miss Sparkes's nephew, a mysterious middle-aged man of reserved deportment who was kept very much in the background. He was never, for example, permitted to meddle with village affairs and was seldom, if ever, to be seen in the street. His duties were severely confined to the large garden that lay behind the little house, a garden that stretched up as far as the wall that separated the potato plots at the backs of the houses from Mile's Hill field.

What a garden it was over which the refined, reticent man presided! In the summer time, if the shop happened to be empty of customers Miss Sparkes would sometimes, as a treat, lead me into this unlikely paradise. There was a small lawn above her green water-butt yard, and at the end of this stood a modest arbor of the kind that John Bunyan might have meditated in—and wonder beyond all wonder, suspended near it, from a pear tree branch, was a large cage containing a talking parrot. . .

Never, never could I hope to express how exciting it used to be to me suddenly to hear the bird's Caribbean screams when it first caught sight of its mistress, slow foot after slow foot, mounting the garden steps. It was a talking parrot—and how its reiterations of 'Pretty Poll,' 'Pretty Poll' would sound shrilly out amongst the wealth of globed peonies, larkspurs, and hollyhocks all in a row. Miss Sparkes, still holding me by the hand, would open the cage door and coax the parrot to sit upon her finger, a fabulous popinjay some of whose feathers were of as pure gold as those I read about in the fairy tales, a gilded emerald bird utterly besotted with love for the old, old woman whose features, indeed, looked not dissimilar to its own, so hooked and headstrong was the nose upon which her spectacles of shining steel were balanced.

Llewelyn Powys

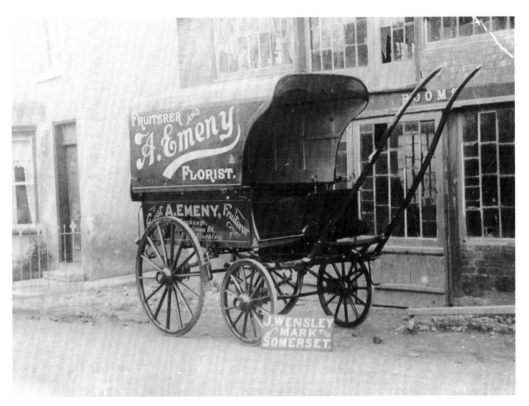

MARK

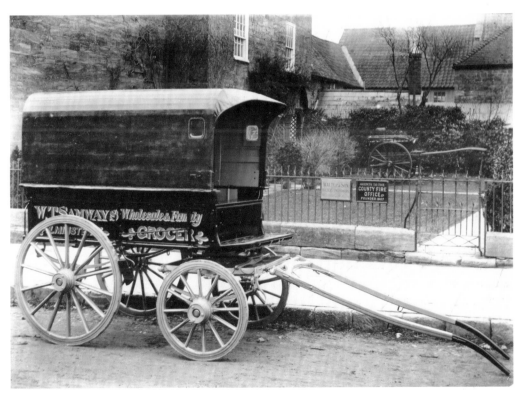

SOUTH PETHERTON

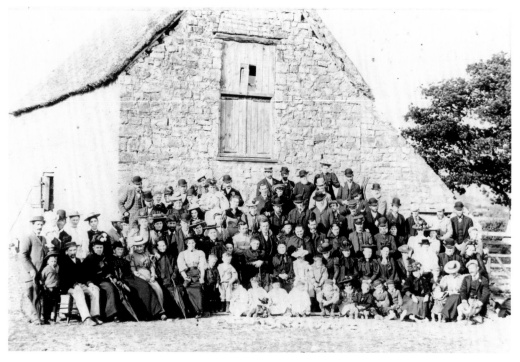

PRIMITIVE METHODISTS MEET AT WALTON

COMING EVENTS

Feb.

1   Teachers' Woodwork and Sloyd class at Sexey's
    Trade School.
    Cary 1st XV v Cheddar, at Cary.
    Non-cons v Tintinhull, at Tintinhtill.

2   Candlemas Day.
    If Candlemas Day be fair and bright,
    Winter will have another fight;
    But if it be dark with clouds and rain,
    Winter is gone, and will not come again.

3   Choral Society.
    School Board meeting.

4   Christian Endeavour.
    Wesley Guild.

5   Lecture on 'The Communion Service' by Revd
    Prebendary Burbidge at 8.15.
    Good Templar Election.

6   Evening Continuation School.

7   Church Choir Practice.

8   Teachers' Woodwork and Sloyd Class at Sexey's
    School.
    Non-cons v Stoke Swifts at Cary.

9   Women's Adult School 3.0; Matthew xvi, 13–28.

10 Choral Society.

11 Evening Continuation School.

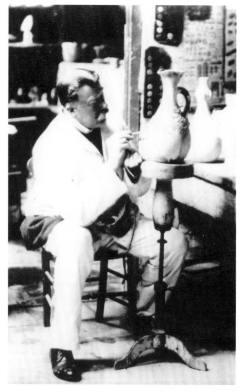

SIR ARTHUR ELTON

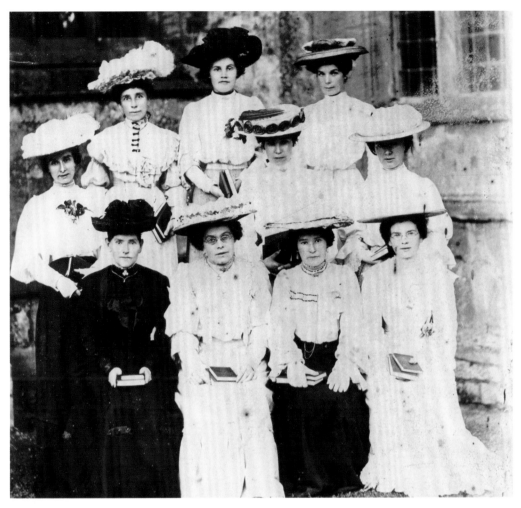

LADY SINGERS, BARRINGTON

Christian Endeavour.

Wesley Guild.

12 Revd Prebendary Burbidge's Lecture at 8.15.

Band of Hope Tea in Wesleyan School-room.

13 Evening Continuation School.

14 Church Choir Practice.

15 Cary 1st XV v Highbridge, at Cary.

Non-cons v Street Rovers at Cary.

Teachers' Woodwork and Sloyd Class at Sexey's School.

16 Be punctual! 9.0; 11.0; 3.0; 6.15; 6.30.

17 Choral Society.

18 Evening Continuation School.

Christian Endeavour.

Wesley Guild.

19 Band of Hope (Wesleyan School).

20 Annual Session of the Mid-Somerset District Lodge, I.O.G.T, in Wesleyan Schoolroom.

Evening Continuation School.

21 Church Choir Practice.

22 Teachers' Woodwork and Sloyd Class at Sexey's School.

Cary 1st XV v Crewkerne at Cary.

23 Men over 20 welcome at Institute 9.0.

24 Choral Society.

25 Evening Continuation School.

Christian Endeavour.

Wesley Guild.

26 Band of Hope 7; Templar Lodge 8.

27 Evening Continuation School.

28 Church Choir Practice.

29 Sloyd class at Sexey's School.

Cary 1st XV v Chard at Chard.

Castle Cary Visitor

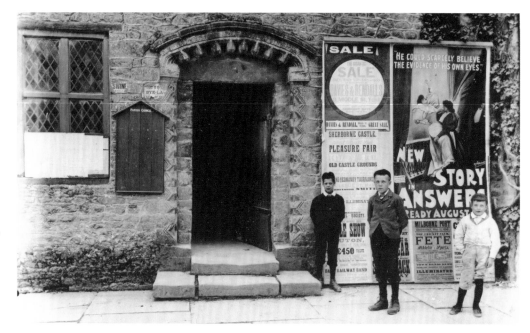

GUILDHALL, MILBORNE PORT

LOCAL EVENTS, 1895–96.

Dec. 25th— 'A Green Christmas.' Between Castle Cary and Hadspen House 14 species of wild flowers were found in bloom.

Dec. 26th—Cricket Club Annual Dance in Town Hall, 8.30 p.m. to 4 a.m. Rumsey's Quadrille Band.

Dec. 27th—Annual Dinner of Liberal Association. Chairman—Mr J.C. Swinburne-Hanham.

Dec. 28th—Attempted suicide by Frank Field.

Dec. 31st—Dance by members of Mr Vaux's class in George Assembly Rooms. Watch-night services at both Chapels.

Jan. 1st—Coffee supper for members of Templar Lodge.

Jan. 2nd—Dance at Alford Assembly Rooms. Christian Endeavour Tea meeting. Mr C.R. Parsons (Bristol) addressed the Men's School Quarterly meeting. Wincanton Assistants defeated Cary Non-cons.

Jan. 4th—Inquest on Frank Field. Cary Non-cons defeated Bruton Reserves.

Jan. 5th—One hundred present at the Adult Schools, men 49, women 51.

Jan. 6th—School Board meeting.

Jan. 7th—Quarterly meeting of the Young Men's Society.

Jan. 8th—S.PG. Lecture by Revd H.M. Joseph, a native of Antigua, on 'Church work in the West Indies.' Lecture illustrated by Lantern Views.

Jan. 9th—Annual Meeting of members of Zion Chapel. Annual meeting Cricket Club (see report).

Jan. 11th—Sexey's Trade School v Cary Non-cons (Drawn), Cary 1st XV defeated Yeovil. Mr Holt-Needham's Harriers met at Manor House.

Jan. 13th—Parish Council meeting. (See Report). Jan. 14th—Liberal Association Annual Meeting.

Jan. 15th—Large attendance at Preb. Burbidge's Lecture.

Jan. 16th—Nearly 50 persons attended Miss Collington's Artisan Cookery Class. Cary Non-cons defeated Wincanton Assistants.

Jan. 18th—Frome 1st XV defeated Cary 1st XV

Jan. 19th—Collections at Adult Schools for the Duke of Westminster's Armenian Fund, realized, £10s. 2d.

Jan. 22th—'Farmer Brown's Awakening' (Lantern Service) at the Band of Hope in Wesleyan School. Tax on Bicycles advocated by Wincanton District Council. An insanitary dwelling at Galhampton condemned.

Castle Cary Visitor

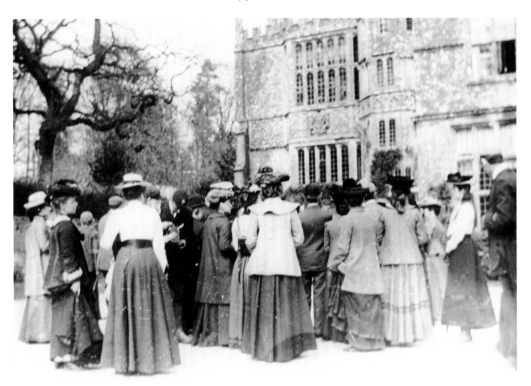

ARCHAEOLOGISTS AND THEIR LADIES, BRYMPTON D'EVERCY

THEY SAY

That a real live Earl is coming to open the Constitutional Club next month.

That 113 Somerset Constables have been awarded St John's Ambulance Certificates in less than two years.

That the Lydford Road wants a few more hundred tons of stone, for the benefit of the traction-engines.

That the Cricket Club has made a large number of fixtures for the coming season.

That a two-days' match has been arranged with the Somerset County Club and Ground, to be played at Cary.

That the Annual Tour will enable the Channel Islanders to see what Cary Cricketers can do.

That *Reynolds' Newspaper*, recently contained some very untruthful references to our town.

That Mr Thring hopes to see the Train-way completed within a few months.

That we are sorry to lose Mr Sessions as a neighbour.

That Court 'True Britons,' A.O.F, is now worth £1,785, and has 162 members.

That Mr Fred Barber's band of juvenile fiddlers recently made a successful debut.

That a freehold property in South Cary Lane is in the market.

That Tramps are too well treated in the Wincanton Union.

That the Steam-roller has been enlivening Bailey Hill, and delighting our small boys.

That Mr Charles Thomas, Senr., is building himself a residence in South Cary.

That the Choral Society loses a model Secretary in Mr C. T. Ellerton.

That our good wishes follow him to Clifton.

That Mr A.J. Mullins will make the Traction Engines pay something more than their Dorset license if he can manage it.

That a large quantity of unfinished gloves were found in a pond at Barrow.

That Mr John Mackie has been elected Secretary of the Choral Society.

Castle Cary Visitor

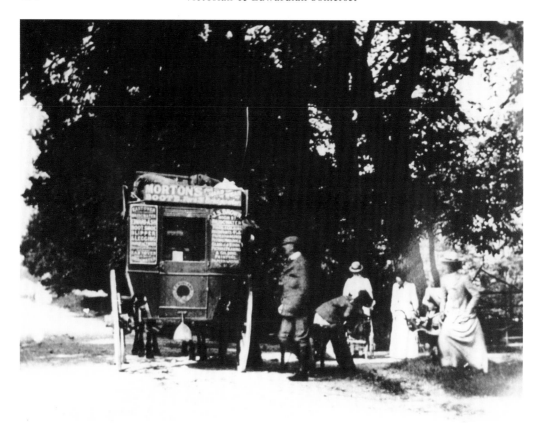

EDINGTON

THE LAND OF ORCHARDS

This is the land of orchards.

Wherever there is a homestead, however small, alongside or behind lies a dark mysterious orchard, running close up to the walls of the farm-buildings and the house. Just a step or two from the back-door, across the garden and through the gate, and you are beneath the trees. The leaning trunks stand all in rows, planted with such care and measured skill that upon whichever side the eye glances it finds a glade. Straight in front, and square upon the right hand and the left, the full breadth opens like a pillared nave; but looking slantways you find narrow alleys leading far away to the tall hedge. The crooked branches arch and, intermingling overhead, shut out the sky; but through the open gaps between the trees fall shafts of sunlight, and through the lattice of the crossing twigs a thousand straggling beams of softer mottled light shoot down to silver the pale lichen on the bark and gild the grasses at your feet. And everywhere dwells a solitude that is not loneliness—a feeling of remoteness from things near at hand akin to the subtle spirit of seclusion that haunts the cloister and the aisle.

The sounds of home and household work, shut off from sight by the thick screen of trees, fall with a constant clearness on the ear—the hasty step of hobnailed soles, the bucket set down sharply on the stones, the clink of a metal handle falling on the rim, and then the creaking rattle of the pump and rushing of the stream.

Sometimes there comes and goes a whistled tune; sometimes the stave of an old song bursts clear and strong from the ripe throat of a full-grown maid. Sometimes a sharp voice calls to 'waste no time.'

Notes and touches such as these go straight to the heart of any contemplative idler out-of-doors. They tell him of the happiness of healthful occupation, the blessing and dignity of honest work—for other folk.

Walter Raymond

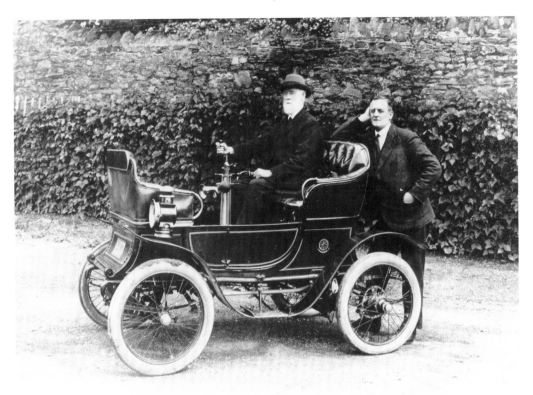

BRIDGWATER'S FIRST CAR

SALTFORD

Saltford is a wayside station on the Great Western Railway well hated no doubt by through travellers whom melancholy fate condemns to 'stopping' trains, and Saltford hill is equally well hated by unskilful drivers on the road to Bristol. But the village itself lies off to the north of road and rail and has no animation thrown into it except for the week preceding the one great day in its calendar, the Bath Regatta on Saltford Reach. The roads are rough and stony and the first building you pass after leaving the station is a mill of stunted build and dilapidated appearance. You come up into the centre of the village and you find that the village inn is no more than a cottage with a sign hung out on its walls, but, on the opposite side of what in a larger place would be considered the market square, is a drinking trough above which some donor has placed a tablet whereon are carved the beautiful words with which our Lord greeted the woman of Samaria at the well—'Whosoever drinketh of this water shall thirst again, but whosoever drinketh of the water that I shall give him shall never thirst, but the water that I shall give him shall be in him a well of water springing up into everlasting life.' No more appropriate inscription for a drinking fountain could be found, but I think a lively interest in the welfare of the people of Saltford would lead to an improvement in the state of the village, would clear the village pound and the little patches of green from the miscellaneous assortment of old tins, panchards and refuse which showed them to be the general rubbish heaps, would improve the narrow rough lane which is the only way to the church and would teach the living more respect for the graves of their ancestors than to allow them to be overgrown with nettles. It was a bleak and cheerless day when I visited Saltford and I do not wish to lay too much stress upon the effect which a certain combination of circumstances may have produced upon an individual, but it did cause a strong feeling of regret in by breast that while some chapel—all honour to it—stood with its doors invitingly open on the main street, the way to the parish church should be up an evidently neglected by-path.

Church Rambler

WATER SUPPLY

Newton is a particularly secluded village. Passengers on the way to Bristol are familiar with the rather striking bridge to which it gives a name, otherwise they might pass to and fro by road or rail a dozen times and be completely unconscious of its existence. But if they will leave the main road just beyond the third milestone from Bath and ascending a steep lane pass the belt of trees which hides the hillside from the road below, they will find a village that very well enjoys its peculiar position. I certainly found one element of advantage in it, as though it was a rainy day when I went there yet thanks to the situation of Newton 'seated on rising ground,' as worthy Mrs Chandler says of Bath, the water ran off the footways and left them passable instead of converting them into quagmires. Emerging from the hill called I believe Smith's hill you face the gates which conceal from you the charming sylvan prospect which the Rectory overlooks. You can proceed right or left along a paved causeway. If you will go to the right you will come to a junction of ways and there in the centre is that ancient and venerable institution, that original temperance hotel—the village pump. But if you go to the left you will perceive at an analogous meeting of ways a drinking place which has been established in obedience to modern requirements, and this consists of a raised basin of red granite which overflows by appointed lips into a second basin below. Mark the progress of civilisation!

Church Rambler

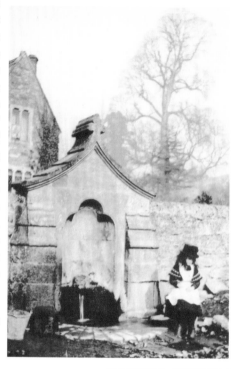

BUCKWELL, DURSTON

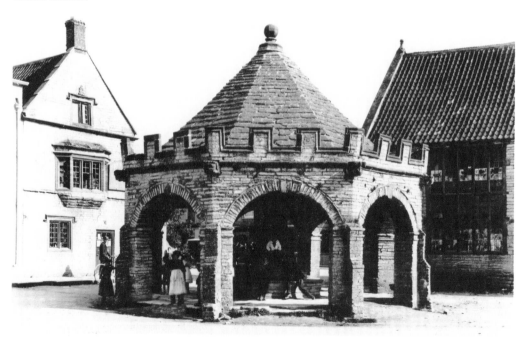

SOMERTON

FROM EXMOOR TO THE QUANTOCKS

Towards even a wind moves among the lengthening shadows, and my footsteps involuntarily seek the glen, where a streamlet trickles down over red flat stones which resound musically as the water strikes them. Ferns are growing so thickly in the hedge that soon it will seem composed of their fronds; the first June rose hangs above their green tips. A water-ousel with white breast rises and flies on; again disturbed, he makes a circle, and returns to the stream behind. On the moist earth there is the print of a hare's pad; here is a foxglove out in flower; and now as the incline rises heather thickens on the slope. Sometimes we wander beside the streamlet which goes a mile into the coombe—the shadow is deep and cool in the vast groove of the hill, the shadow accumulates there, and is pressed by its own weight—up slowly as far as the 'sog,' or peaty place where the spring rises, and where the sundew grows. Sometimes climbing steep and rocky walls—scarce sprinkled with grass—we pause every other minute to look down on the great valley which reaches across to Dunkery. The horned sheep, which are practically wild, like wild creatures have worn out holes for themselves to lie in beside the hill. If resolution is strong, we move through the dark heather (soon to be purple), startling the heath-poults, or black game, till at last the Channel opens, and the far-distant Flat and Steep Holms lie, as it looks, afloat on the dim sea. This is labour enough; stern indeed must be the mind that could work at summer's noon in Somerset, when the apple vineyards slumber; when the tall foxgloves stand in the heavy heat, and the soft air warms the deepest day-shadow so that nothing is cool to the touch but the ferns. Is there anything so good as to do nothing?

Richard Jefferies

TARR STEPS

Some of the trout came up from under Torre-steps, a singular structure which here connects the shores of the stream. Every one has seen a row of stepping stones across a shallow brook; now pile other stones on each of these, forming buttresses, and lay flat stones like unhewn planks from buttress to buttress, and you have the plan of this primitive bridge. It has a megalithic appearance, as if associated with the age of rude stone monuments. They say its origin is doubtful; there can be no doubt of the loveliness of the spot.

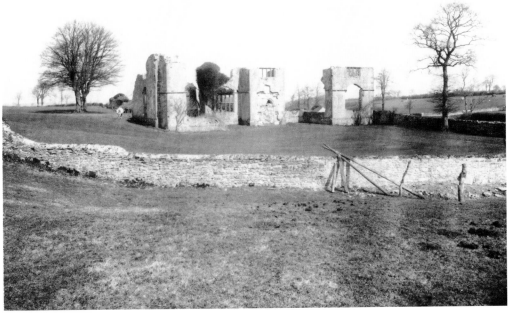

WHATLEY

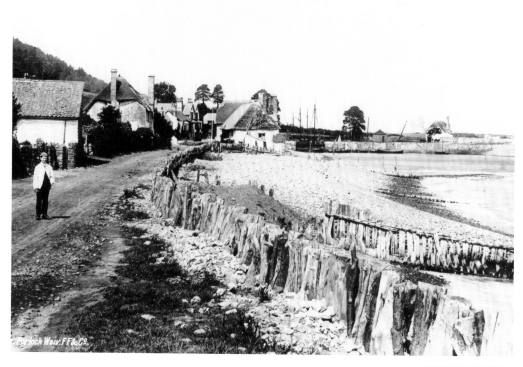

PORLOCK WEIR

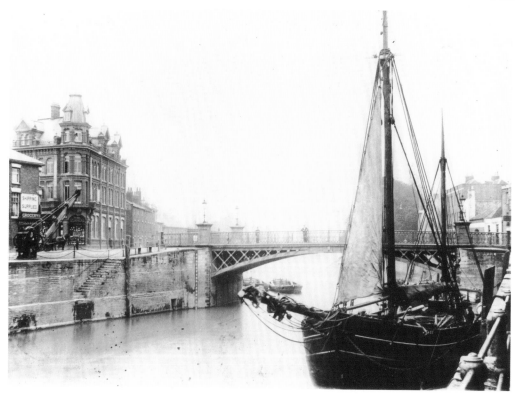

BRIDGWATER

The Barle comes with his natural rush and fierceness under the unhewn stone planking, then deepens, and there overhanging a black pool—for the shadow was so deep as to be black—grew a large bunch of marsh marigolds in fullest flower, the broad golden cups almost resting on the black water. The bridge is not intended for wheels, and though it is as firm as the rock, foot passengers have to look at their steps, as the great planks, flecked with lichen at the edges, are not all level. The horned sheep and lambs go over it—where do they not go? Like goats they wander everywhere.

Richard Jefferies

OUR PARISH COUNCIL

April 19th, 1895—Messrs Mackie, Moore, R.H. White, Lydford, Whitelock, and H. Harrold, were appointed a subcommittee to inspect the Sewage Works from time to time on behalf of the Parochial Committee.

July 26th—At the Council meeting on this date Gaslighting came in for considerable attention. A letter from the Charity Commissioners was read. Messrs Jas. Mackie and Harry Harrold were elected trustees of Lewis's Bread Charity. Sewage Works reported to be in satisfactory order.

August 26th—The Council decided to ask for £100 for Street Lighting. The Gas Company had raised the charge per lamp from £1 11s. 6d. to £1 15s. The sum asked for was subsequently voted by a Parish Meeting after a good deal of discussion.

January 13th, 1896—The chairman read a letter from the Ansford Parish Council asking the Cary Council to join them in a petition to the Great Western Railway Company to erect a footbridge at the Castle Cary station, which is in Ansford parish. This led to a discussion as to the possibility of getting the company to build a new station nearer the town, the present station being more than a mile away, and a rumour having been circulated that a new station was in contemplation in connection with the proposed new line to Langport. Eventually it was unanimously agreed to ask the company to consider the practicability of bringing the station nearer the town, and failing this to construct a footbridge or subway at the existing station, the danger and inconvenience of the present level crossing being fully recognised by the council.

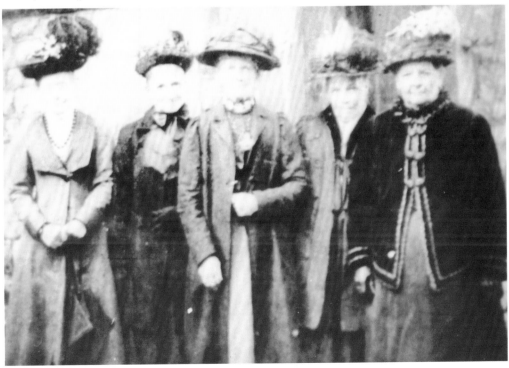

BANWELL LADIES

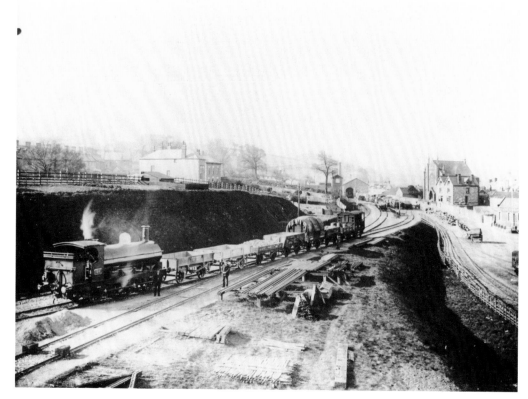

WATCHET

Several complaints as to footpaths and pavements in the parish were brought forward by members, and in the case of a pathway at Clanville it was decided to call the attention of the surveyor to its dangerous condition. The council afterwards sat as the Parochial Committee. The sub-committee for superintending the sewage works were asked for a report, but they had held no meeting for some time—Several individual members of the committee, however, stated that they had recently visited the works, and found them in a very neglected state—After some discussion it was arranged that the sub-committee should meet at the works on Wednesday afternoon, and that the Parochial Committee should be called together subsequently to receive their report.

Castle Cary Visitor

TRADITION

By a farmer's door I found a tall branch of oak lying against the porch. The bark was dry, and the leaves were shrivelled, but the bough had been originally taken green from the tree. These boughs are discovered against the door on the morning of the 29th of May, and are in memory of the escape of King Charles from his enemies by hiding in an oak. The village ringers leave them, and then go to the church and ring a peal, for which they expect cider or small coin from each loyal person honoured with an oak-branch. Another custom, infinitely more ancient, is that of singing to the apple-trees in early spring, so that the orchards may be induced to bear a good crop. The singers come round and visit each orchard; they have a rhyme specially for the purpose, part of the refrain of which is that a cup of good cider cannot do any one harm, a hint which brings out a canful. In strange contrast to these genial customs, which accord so well with flowery fields, I heard an instance of the coldest indifference. An old couple lived for many years in a cottage; at last the wife died, and the husband, while the body was in the house, had his meals on the coffin as a table.

Richard Jefferies

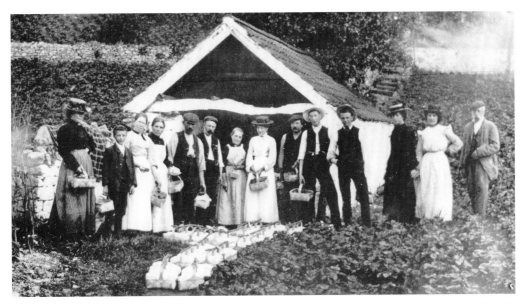

STRAWBERRY PICKING, CHEDDAR

APPLE PICKING

By midsummer the trees are covered one and all in a mantle of green. The eye at first can scarcely distinguish the new-kerned fruit from the leaves; and so it lasts until, as ripeness slowly gilds and reddens the full-grown crop, the orchard blazes forth in a splendour of plenty most beautiful to behold.

Everywhere the apples shine and glisten in the sun. There are some of amber, some of gold, and some with streaks that look like blood. There is also an old-world variety, excellent for cider, that puts on a sort of purple redness, rich and dull like velvet, but clinging so thick and close to every spray that the tree becomes clad in an imperial robe. Soon it casts its largess all around. The ground grows ruddy with the fallen fruit, and from the wood four fields away, now and again, a stately pheasant, straying along the hedgerows, finds his way close to the homestead walls. Then he comes there every day, fraternises with the farm-yard fowls, and stalks about under the trees, for a pheasant is fond of apples and dearly loves the pips.

Then the apple-picking comes very soon.

Armed with long ashen poles the folk come out from house, the youth who whistled and the maid who sang. They rattle down the fruit from the topmost branch, pick it up in baskets, and pile it into a heap ready for the cart to carry it to the poundhouse to be ground for making cider. It is the last harvest of the year. The Indian summer yields and flees before advancing frost. The autumn orchard leaves, brighter at fall than they have ever been, turn colour, grow thin, and shiver in the wind. Soon there is nothing left but a sprinkling of stray yellow pippins clinging to the naked branches.

In olden times, after the picking was done, the village folk used to come gleaning for those apples that remained. They called it 'pixy-wording.' They used to say the fairies held them on the trees to make a hoard; and although they look so sparse and few, these stragglers, put together, make up what the good souls of Somerset call 'a tidy vew.' But pixies are gone, and pixy-worders too. The last forgotten apples remain to drop off with the wind; and then once more you need look for nothing but the glean of winter sunshine upon the trees..

Walter Raymond

MEMORY

Fame travels slowly up these breathless hills, and pauses overcome in the heated hollow lanes. A famous wit of European reputation, when living, resided in Somerset. A traveller one day chancing to pass through the very next parish inquired of a local man if somebody called Sydney Smith did not once live in that neighbourhood.

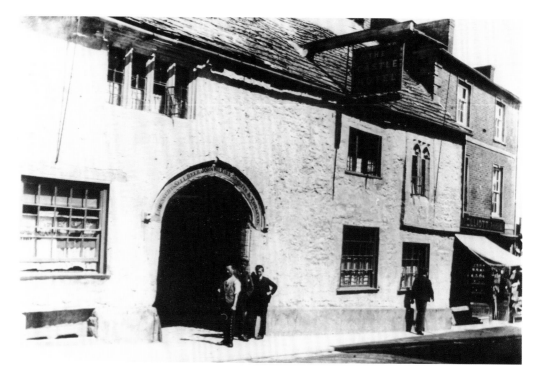

YEOVIL

'Yes,' was the reply, 'I've heard all about Sydney Smith; I can tell you. He was a highwayman and was hung on that hill there.' He would have shown the very stump of the gallows-tree as proof positive, like Jack Cade's bricks, alive in the chimney to this day.

There really was a highwayman, however, whose adventures are said to have suggested Lorna Doone. This desperate fellow had of course his houses of call, where he could get refreshment safely, on the moors. One bitter winter's day the robber sat down to a hearty dinner in an inn at Exford. Placing his pistols before him, he made himself comfortable, and ate and drank his fill. By and by, an old woman entered, and humbly took a seat in a corner far from the fire. In time the highwayman observed the wretched, shivering creature, and of his princely generosity told her to come and sit by the hearth. The old woman gladly obeyed, and crouched beside him. Presently, as he sat absorbed in his meal, his arms were suddenly pinioned from behind. The old woman had him tight so that he could not use his weapons, while at a call constables, who had been posted about, rushed in and secured him. The old woman was in fact a man in disguise. A relation of the thief-taker still lives and tells the tale. The highwayman's mare, mentioned in the novel, had been trained to come at his call, and was so ungovernable that they shot her.

Richard Jefferies

FOOTBALL

The season of 1894–95 will always occupy a prominent position in the history of the Castle Cary Football Club. In fact it is very doubtful if such a brilliant record will ever be equalled. During the whole season only three tries were scored against the club, and only one match lost, that being against Martock, a team which had never before beaten Cary. Eight matches were won, five drawn, and only the one defeat referred to. Two victories were registered against Langport, and one each against Yeovil, Frome, Bath, Wells, Martock, and Crewkerne, whilst matches against Weymouth (twice), Crewkerne, Frome, and Yeovil were left drawn.

The present season, 1895–96, has been attended with only moderate success, but this may be accounted for by the fact that of nine matches played, only two have been contested on our own ground, both of which we

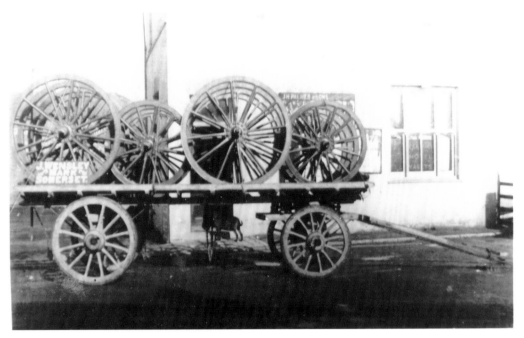

MARK

have won. The opening match with Cheddar was drawn—no score. Crewkerne next were encountered, and Cary suffered defeat by 12 points to *nil*. A good win at Wells followed this, but the following week Cary went down rather badly before the King's School, Sherborne. Yeovil also proved victorious over our XV, on their ground, but wins against Frome here, and Highbridge at Highbridge, brought 1895 to a close.

The football of the month consists of two matches only. The first of these, against Yeovil, has always been regarded as the 'Match of the Season,' and the fixture drew a large concourse of spectators, who were subsequently delighted to witness the triumph of the Cary team over their opponents by the substantial score of 8 points to *nil*, thus wiping out the reverse suffered at Yeovil earlier in the season. I have before me as I write a report of the first match played against Yeovil in 1888, one paragraph reads thus: 'The Cary team having studied the rules, and practised frequently, will prove formidable opponents some day.' How true has been the prophecy, for today Cary are Yeovil's keenest rivals, and no fixture on their programme attracts more interest than the meeting of the two teams.

The return match with Frome, on their ground, resulted in the defeat of Cary by one try to nil, although I have the authority of the Frome papers that the best team lost.

JOHN MACKIE

Castle Cary Visitor

KEYNSHAM FIRE ENGINE

Well as the church has been restored it appeared to me from the state of the windows when I visited it that it has not yet been made weather-tight, and it struck me that the house of God is not treated with that reverent care which we expect. I walked round the churchyard and I was never in a worse kept one. There was no path round the church, but grass and nettles had been allowed to grow across the graves and everywhere else so that in some places I was literally knee deep in them. Then too I found that the beautiful porch is thought worthy of no better purpose than to shelter the fire-engine. Is not the parish wealthy enough to find some shed to cover this useful machine without desecrating the parish church? Against the side of the porch there is a wooden shanty to serve as a coal-cellar for the heating apparatus.

Church Rambler

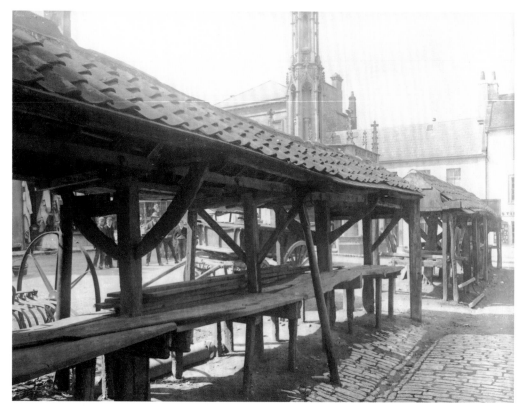

SHAMBLES, SHEPTON MALLET

I COME TO HAWKESCOMBE

In Somerset there are miles and miles of wild country high on the hills which seem too remote for the ordinary visitor to reach. But the tiny villages which nestle in its combes hold treasures of beauty little dreamed of by those who pass them by. I speak not only of things, but of human lives, and think of my own village, Hawkescombe.

From the summit of its highest hill, some nine hundred feet above sea-level, over which buzzards often circle, the view is wonderful. The range of which this height forms part is in the shape of a crescent, or sickle, with its back humped up against north and north-east winds which otherwise would sweep upon the village without a check over miles and miles of lowlands. To the east are the Mendips, many miles away, and north-west lie the Blackdowns with the Vale of Taunton just below. A near cluster of red roofs marks Hawkescombe's market town. The rich country between it and the village has many streams fringed with loose-strife, willow-herb, meadowsweet, and forget-me-not, and its meadows of bright emerald green are spangled in their seasons with cowslips, oxlips, and wild orchids. The copses seen here and there are carpeted in spring and summer with Lent-lilies, primroses, violets, anemones, bluebells, and foxgloves. The ploughed fields are splendid with rich, warm, old red sandstone and marl.

On one high knap the badger earths are. It stands as a sentinel for the great wood of heavy forest timber, oak, ash, chestnut, and pine, which falls away below it to the river. To the west a purple fringe marks Exmoor, and in the bite of the hills the Bristol Channel gleams like a jewel. Between it and Hawkescombe a hanging larchwood is where the woodcock breeds. The high down to the north is where I last saw a honey buzzard, and in the field below I found, only last season, a quail nestling.

It is a great country for birds. On the far sea cliffs are ravens; yes, and a peregrine's eyrie. The golden commons of gorse and broom and bracken have thickets of brambles sacred to the red-backed shrike and scolding chats. Far below Hawkescombe hill one moss-grown peaty bog, carpeted with spagnum moss, with

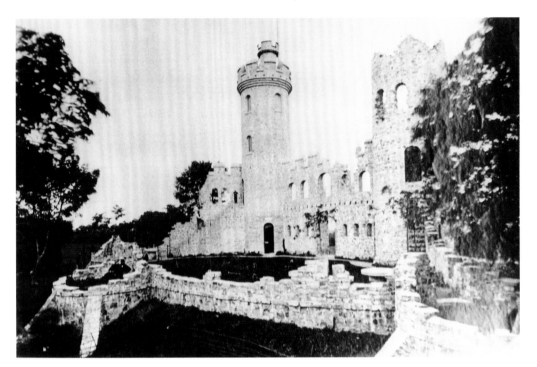

KNOWLE 'CASTLE', BAWDRIP

patches of marsh-marigold, iris, and bulrush, is the breeding-ground of snipe, and the lane running along two sides of it, with overgrown and tangled hedges which are a smother of honeysuckle and old man's beard, is a veritable heaven of warblers. The bubbling burn which divides our parish from the next is full of trout and a haunt of dippers.

What brought me here to Hawkescombe? In what appeared to me an evil hour the 'medicine men' forbade me to hold a parish of my own. They laid me on the shelf. And yet, as they still allowed me to do a little work, I could regard myself as in harness, rather than as permanently turned out to grass. Somerset was the county in which I decided to find a home, for it is one with many parsons, struggling in scattered parishes, who need help badly. It affords unrivalled opportunities for the indulgence in leisure hours of my youthful hobby, natural history. And it is rich, as I have long since proved, in the very kindest, most ingenuous, and lovable of country folk. I love it, every bit of it: and I love them, every one of them!

I realised with trepidation that I was coming a stranger among strangers, and that I might, too, easily run counter to Hawkescolnbe's ancient traditions. But very soon the villagers made all plain to us. The foundations of village life had been well and truly laid of old on the rock of mutual loving service and respect, and the spirit of real neighbourliness still persisted, only needing reverent protection against frost to render the fabric as secure as ever. The whole atmosphere breathed loyalty and affection. Not that they are a folk who wear their hearts upon their sleeves! With them appearance goes for little, and profession even less; they watch and read between the lines; are overshrewd at sucking the marrow-bone of motive dry, and seldom make a bad mistake in judgment. Which means, of course, that they are slow to change or be convinced. But once satisfied, they trust; the battle's won and nothing is withheld.

The village lies hidden from the busy world. Those who pass along the high road might never know of its existence. But if they left it, and, passing by the sandpits, alive with martins sailing in and out of their burrows, went down the side of this wood, where we come to listen to the woodlark's song of an evening, then they would come upon Hawkescombe. Brooding over all below, and standing out from among the limes and yew trees, is the splendid old church tower of Hamhill stone, toned and weathered to lovely gold and russets. By the lych-gate stands the ancient preaching cross. The rectory is near, but hidden in the trees. A step beyond

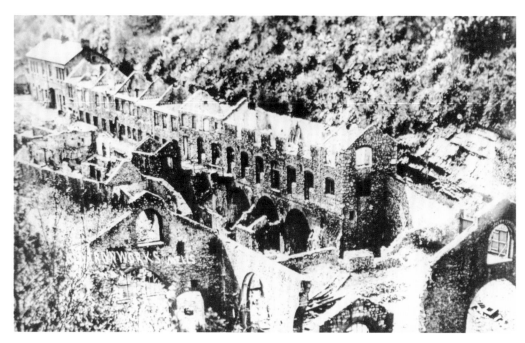

FUSSELLS' IRON WORKS

the church gives a glimpse of the grey stone gables of the Manor House, my shelf. From there the zigzag road winds its halting way downhill, across the stream, and by easier stages creeps up the farther side of the valley. The cottages sprinkled on either side of it are stone built and mostly roofed with thatch, in the more exposed situations with stone field slates, while here and there is a bit of wall or barton built of red mud or wattle.

There is not a cottage that I do not know. Close to the church is the humble but beautiful dwelling of Jim and Martha Webb. It was Jim who buried his master's charger as near the church as might be. And if a tubby figure is ever seen by the lych-gate or the ancient preaching cross, it will be that of our parish clerk and sexton, Ben Brindle, always thirsting for a gossip. An oval patch of emerald green is the cricket ground, where Brace, the keeper, and his arch-enemy Knight, the poacher, made the great catch which should become historic. From the cricket ground the road winds down across a stream, and, half-way, a white cottage, gleaming against a clump of dark pines, is the house of crazy 'Ria'. Beyond it stands Fuchsia Cottage, where I have often tried in vain to get a word in edgeways with Louisa Knibb. The farm near it is owned by Levi Keitch, explorer of the milky way, to put it so. The cottage at the cross-roads is where dear Letty Marchant, our wild dancer, had the trouble of her life solved. Upon the very crest of Stooper's Knapp is the home of 'Rickety' Rickman, the village cobbler, and dear old Jenny his wife, who will 'tell' with me no more. The rocky downs to the west are sacred to the profound philosophy and ethics of our splendid shepherd, Silas Noldart. With glasses can be seen beyond the downs a dark outcrop of rock standing up against the evening sky, and just beneath it a brown speck, like a mole on a man's chin, which was the house of Pat Lambert, the outcast. Away south, in a fold of the downs, dwell the notable churchwarden, Sam Barton, and his neighbour, that voluble old seaman, Peter Austin, an equally interesting upholder of law and order. That derelict farmstead standing alone in the bottom once housed Philip Creech, whose last will and testament may cost some pains to decipher. That is the house of 'Appy, the carter, a man of one great speciality, and not far from it is dear old John Gobbler's forge, the shrine of many memories.

All these wild open moors and bracing downs stretched out before us breed a splendid race of hill-folk proud of their descent, and of somewhat plain and open speech. Yet I love them, and they know it; how much I owe them they will never know.

Alfred Percivall

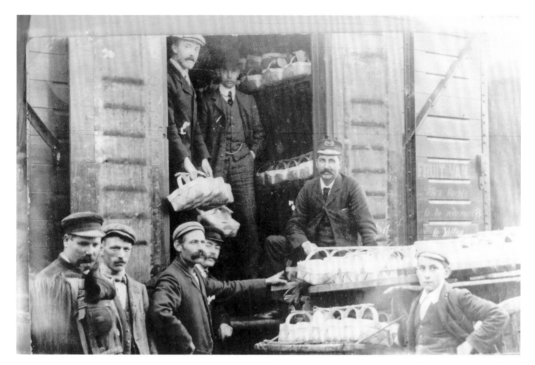

LOADING STRAWBERRIES ON TO THE TRAIN

CLEVEDON: A LITERARY SHRINE

Clevedon town, with its tall houses of grey stone, its new church standing high, its Franciscan friary, its steep white streets, its gardens and fields, and its long curving line of cliffs reaching to Portishead, makes a pleasant picture darkly framed by encircling hills, some with their summits crowned by tree-clusters, others with thickly-wooded sides, and a few bare, rugged, and brown. On the opposite side of the Channel are the Welsh hills, a misty blue melting in the distance, with here and there a sharp peak piercing the sky. Gazing seawards you may detect far down the river a small tongue of land protruding into the water, or a jutting cliff, or a rocky islet around which the waves make a white and glistening ring of foam, while a lighthouse stands forth gauntly in mid-water like a giant sentinel. Looking inland again you see behind the little town a looming hill of fir, ever crowded with shadows, and where, for those who know the tale, the pale ghosts of memory linger away. In the bosom of the wood lies the stately Elizabethan mansion, the ancestral home of the Hallams and Eltons, undiscovered until many a winding walk has been traversed among the multitudinous trees, and until the heights of the land have been laboriously scaled. It was among these quiet hills and valleys, in a sparsely-peopled country, that the first and last scenes were played in one of the most sadly-beautiful of human dramas—a drama solemn and tragic, which closed with the death of a young man of rare genius, of surpassing powers, of attributes that have been called divine; a short drama of life and death, which gained for its epilogue the most beautiful elegy and requiem in the English language, perhaps in the world, the 'In Memoriam' of his friend, Alfred Tennyson.

Clevedon has other poetical associations. Here came Coleridge in 1795, a young man with a young wife, living in poverty, poetry, and dreams. Perhaps his sojourn in Somersetshire constituted the happiest days of his life, for he had not yet learnt how hostile the world can be to genius, how indifferent to merit, how ungrateful to its benefactors; and how, while it raises monuments to the dead, it ignores the living.

When Coleridge died the world was proud to claim him, to honour and revere his name, to award him a place among the illustrious. But it was only in his little Rose Cottage at Clevedon and at Nether Stowey that he was truly happy and in comfort, for he saw the golden promise of the future: he saw the 'distant Eden gleam,' knowing not (like the weary traveller in the desert craving a haven of rest) that the light was but that of the

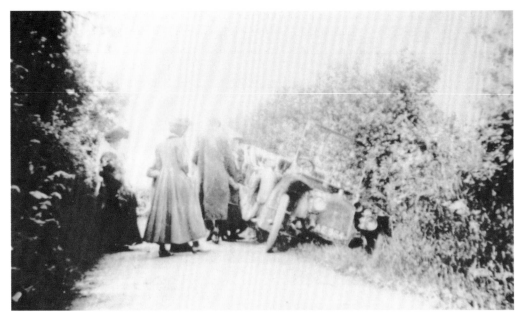

MR HOBHOUSE'S CAR, SMALL DOWN CAMP

deceptive mirage which brings madness and despair. Mr Hall Caine tells us of Coleridge's home at Clevedon that it was 'a pretty little place, one storey high, with a rose-tree peeping in at the chamber window. The parlour was whitewashed, but then the rent was only five pounds a year.' We owe to Coleridge's residence in this summer-land many a bright and joyous poem which reflects the contentment and placidity of the poet's mind.

There are the stanzas composed while climbing Brockley Coombe, the opening lines of the poem, 'Fear in Solitude,' and some distinct references in that beautiful composition called 'The Æolian Harp.' He spoke in after years with tender regret of the 'pretty cot' where the tallest rose 'peeped at the chamber window;' while the whole country was a constant delight to him with its

> Many steepled track magnificent
> Of hilly fields and meadows, and the sea
> With some fair barque, perhaps, whose sails light up
> The slip of smooth clear blue betwixt two isles
> Of purple shadow.

Thus, had there been no Hallam, Clevedon would have been enchanted ground, but now it has become a shrine. The little river-side town, a summer haunt, possesses a sad attraction for the student of Tennyson. While Coleridge sang its charms, Tennyson has endued it with solemn interest. Here Arthur Hallam was born, here he was visited by his friend, here he was brought dead—

> The Danube to the Severn gave
> The darken'd heart that beat no more;

—here his tablet, bearing the tribute of a mourning but resigned father, 'glimmers to the morn,' and was the constant vision of the man who loved him.

To the eyes of the reverent pilgrim all things are changed: their fairness is sad, and their sweetness breathes only of the lamentable, devastating past. Every hill and coppice, every sunlit vale, and every gliding stream, recall to memory as by conjuration the lost and long-past days when the two young poets, knit in the indissoluble bonds of friendship and affinity, wandered together in the promise of life, matured their schemes, and launched their hopes upon a wrecking sea. The one was foredoomed by fate, and the survivor remained to question the laws and their framer upon the justice of human destiny. Scarcely had Arthur Hallam advanced his first steps and made his merit known, than he was stricken down by 'the spectre fear'd of man'; and the other, burdened with a sorrow knowing no surcease, was left alone on a desolate shore.

Cuming Walters

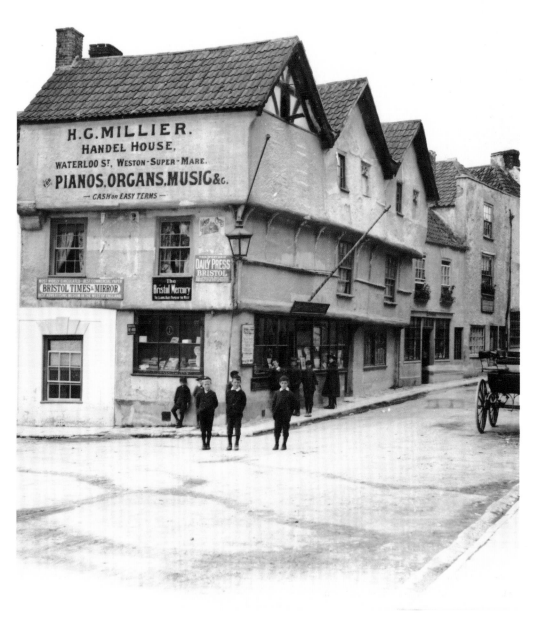

AXBRIDGE

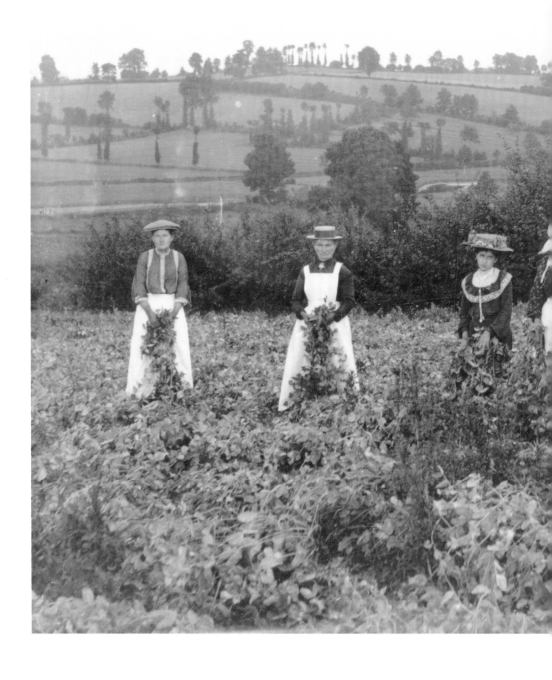

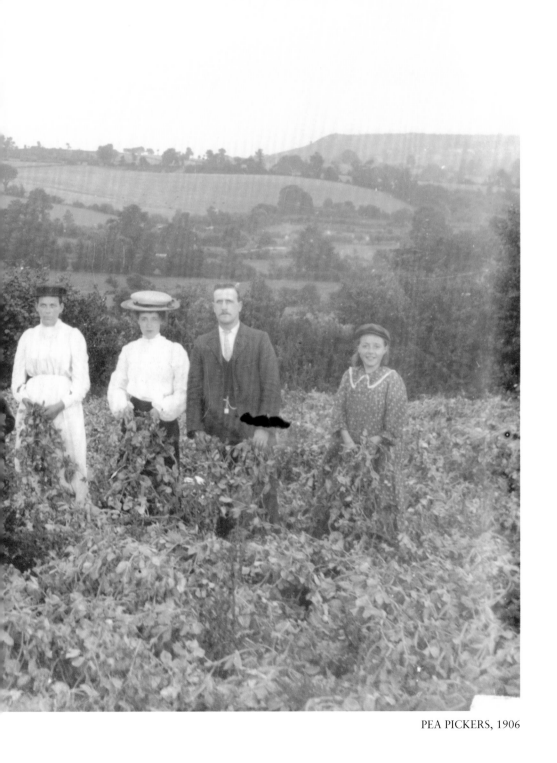

PEA PICKERS, 1906

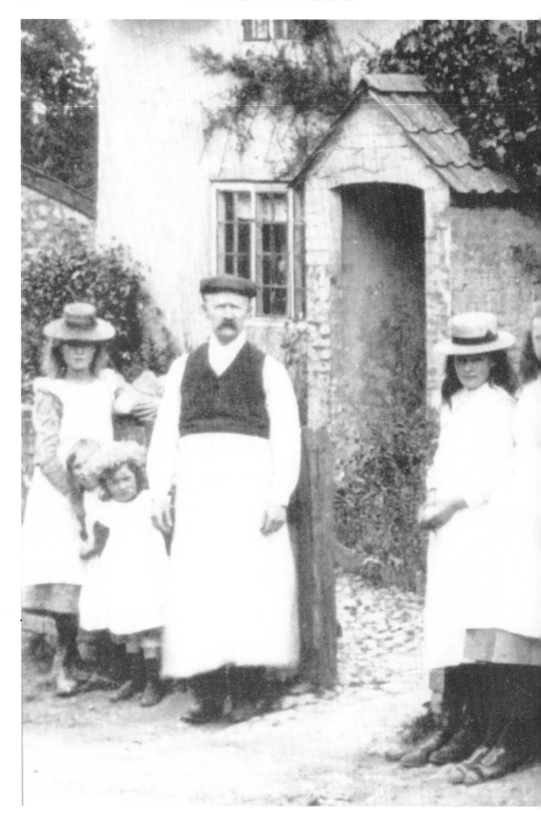

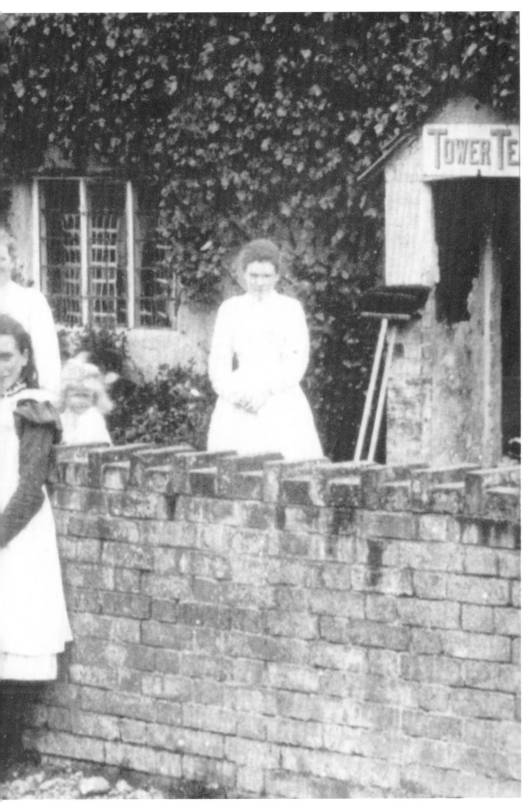

STOKE SUB HAMDON

SOURCES, PHOTOGRAPHIC DETAILS AND ACKNOWLEDGEMENTS

TEXT

The page numbers given below relate to this book and not to the page numbers of the source hooks.

Printed books: Anon, 'A Village School', *Macmillan's Magazine*; *Castle Cary Visitor*, January 1896; Armistead Cay (editor), *The Mayorality of George Woodiwiss. Esq., J.P., D.L., Mayor of Bath* 1896–7; *The Church Rambler* (1876–7); Theodore Compton, *Winscombe Sketches amongst the Mendip Hills* (2nd edition 1882), pp. 45–8; W. Cook, *Zummersetshire Rhymes*; F. G. Hearth, *The 'Romance' of Peasant Life in the West of England* (1872); Richard Jefferies, 'Summer in Somerset', *English Illustrated Magazine* (1888); John Jolliffe (editor), *Raymond Asquith: Life and Letters* (1980); *Journal of the British Dairy Farmers Association viii* (1893); Francis Kilvert, *Kilvert's Diary*, edited William Plomer; Percy Lovell (editor), *Somerset Anthology: twenty-four pieces by Roger Clarke of Street* 1871-1961 (1975); Alfred Percivall (the Revd. Alfred Percivall Pott); *Somerset Neighbours* (1921; Llewellyn Powys, *A Baker's Dozen* (1941); *Somerset Essays* (1937); Charles A.M. Press, *In the Verdant West* (1890); Walter Raymond, in *The Idler*; in *New Liberal Review* (June 1901); Cuming Walters, *Bygone Somerset* (1897); *Western Gazette Almanac*, 1898; H. Hay Wilson, *A Somersetshire Sketchbook* (1902).

Manuscript sources: Diary of the Revd S.W. Baker, vicar Of Mulchelney (Somerset Record Office D/P/much 23/ 1); Diary of the Revd S.H.A. Hervey, vicar of Wedmore (typescript III possession of the editor.

ILLUSTRATIONS

The following credits and information on photographs used in the book are given in ascending page order. Where a source is frequently cited it is referred to by its initials only (key at end of credits list).

PHOTOGRAPHERS

Most of the photographers whose work appears in this volume are unknown. The work of professionals like W H. Davis of Bath, Robert Gillo of Bridgwater, H.H. Hole of Williton, W Morley of Taunton, T.W Phillips of Wells and, of course, Francis Frith will be known to many, and among the amateurs the work of Sydney Vaux of Seavington St Mary stands the test of time. Many of these photographs are taken from glass plates in the large collection of the Somerset Archaeological and Natural History Society, in whose care the executors of several former members have deposited the exposures of a lifetime. It is much to be regretted that as yet full credit for their work cannot be accurately ascribed, although at least some of the work of Dr F.J. Allen of Shepton Mallet and Cambridge can be recognized. More of the anonymous plates may well be the work of Dr Allen, and yet others, possibly a majority, are probably the work of H. St George Gray, for many years assistant secretary of the Archaeological Society. Allen and Gray were, of course, amateurs with particular antiquarian interests. Other amateurs, with rather more domestic and family interests in view, provide a necessary balance, and the albums of families such as the Bristers, the Duckworths, the Hams, the Nutts and the Southcombes enable the historian to reach a little nearer to the life of ordinary people so graphically described in the accompanying texts.

ACKNOWLEDGEMENTS

Anyone who compiles a book of this kind incurs many debts. I thank Rosemary Prudden for expertly arranging a mass of texts and prints into proper order. To the staff of the Somerset Record Office, and especially to Tom Mayberry, I am grateful for help in selection, and to Tom for so expertly copying them; similarly to the staff of the Somerset Museum Service, especially Ann Healey and Mary Grvspeerdt for selection help and Laurence Bostock for his photographic skills; to David Bronlwich for suggesting textual sources and for copy printing; to Basil Searle and Geoff Roberts for printing from the glass plates; and to Jeremy Dunning for printing my own negatives.

My sincere thanks are due to the Somerset Archaeological and Natural History Society, to the Somerset County Museums Service, the Somerset Library Service, and the Somerset Archive and Record Service for permission to reproduce material in their ownership or custody. I am most grateful to the following owners or depositors of material: Andrew Bve, the executors of the late J.A. Clark, John Cornwell, the executors of the late Arthur Duckworth, the Revd Adrian Hallett, Mr Ham, the Revd Derek House, Adrian Moon, the National Rivers Authority, H.R. Nutt, Taunton Deane Borough Council, Miss G. Willis. The extract from the letter of Raymond Asquith appears by permission of the Hon. John Jolliffe.